A PERVERSE HISTORY
OF THE HUMAN
HEART

A PERVERSE HISTORY
OF THE HUMAN
HEART

MILAD DOUEIHI

HARVARD UNIVERSITY PRESS
Cambridge, Massachusetts
London, England
1997

This work was previously published as *Histoire Perverse
du Coeur Humain* in the series La Librairie du XXe Siècle,
edited by Maurice Olender.
Copyright © 1996 by Les Editions du Seuil.

Library of Congress Cataloging-in-Publication Data

Doueihi, Milad.
[Histoire perverse du coeur humain. English]
A perverse history of the human heart / Milad Doueihi.
p. cm.
Includes bibliographical references and index.
ISBN 0-674-66325-X (cloth : alk. paper). —
ISBN 0-674-66327-6 (pbk. : alk. paper)
1. Heart in literature. 2. Cannibalism in literature.
3. Literature—History and criticism. I. Title.
PN56.H374D68 1997
809'.9336—dc21   97-27437

Designed by Gwen Nefsky Frankfeldt

For Wilda, with all my love

Contents

Contents

Illustrations

Above all else guard your heart,
For it is the wellspring of life.

PROVERBS 4:23

Introduction

But my companions at one of Sossius Senecio's dinners suspected me of being committed to the beliefs of the Orphics
and Pythagoreans and holding the egg taboo, as some hold the
heart and brain, because I thought it to be the first principle
of creation. And Alexander the Epicurean teasingly recited:
Now eating the beans is much like eating parents' heads. For
these people call eggs "beans" *(kuamoi)*, punning on the word
conception *(kuesis)*, and they think that eating eggs in no way
differs from using the creatures which produce the eggs.

PLUTARCH, *MORALIA*

This book tells part of the story and the history of the human
heart from the early Greek period down to the early modern
period. By doing so, it traces the various textual and cultural
representations of the status and function of the human heart in
a number of mythological, theological, and literary texts. In the
majority of the texts I will examine in the book, the heart is not
only considered a privileged and unique organ of the human
body, it is also an organ that is often, and at times in a brutal
and violent fashion, made into an edible object that is either eaten

by the person or persons who murder their victim or, more frequently, offered, in disguise, as food to a third party.

What is it about the heart and its symbolic powers that makes it into such an attractive and perverse offering? What is so specific to the heart that allows its transformation into food? What special characteristics of the heart inform the mechanisms of substitution and identification that are involved in the gesture of offering the human heart as human food? Finally, how can we trace the changing representations of the human heart in its unfortunate journey from the central organ of the human body to becoming that which is eaten and consumed by that body?

In order to begin answering some of these questions, it is appropriate to sketch briefly the history of the heart and its place in the mythological, philosophical, and medical literatures of ancient Greece. In this context, I will provide a brief survey of the representations of the heart in some Greek texts and their Christian and medieval descendants and then a discussion of an ancient Egyptian literary tale that is, at least to my knowledge, the first text that portrays the human heart in a story that ties together sexuality, death, rebirth, and regeneration—themes that I will discuss throughout this book.

An Organ Like No Other

In the Orphic and Pythagorean theologies, the heart lies at the center of the prohibition against the eating of flesh. It also occupies a privileged and unique position in the articulation of their theories of rebirth and regeneration of the soul. According to Plutarch: "Human souls are imprisoned in mortal bodies as a punishment for murder, the eating of animal flesh, and cannibalism. This doctrine, however, seems to be even older, for the stories told about the sufferings and dismemberment of Dionysus and the outrageous assaults of the Titans upon him, and their punishment and blasting by thunderbolt after they had tasted his blood—all this is a myth which in its inner meaning has to do with rebirth. For to that faculty in us which is unreasonable and disordered and violent, and does not come from the gods, but from evil spirits, the ancients gave the name Titans."[1] Thus, at the origin of the Orphic and Pythagorean valorization of the heart, we find the story of the sacrifice of the child Dionysus. The Titans, the first creatures of the earth, kidnap the child Dionysus. They then proceed to murder him, dissecting his body, boiling and broiling his tender flesh. Once the flesh of the young god has been thus prepared, they eat it. But before they can consume his heart, they are killed by Zeus' lightning, and the young god is reborn and regenerated from his heart.

The story of the sacrifice and dismemberment of Dionysus is taken to represent the evils of eating human or animal flesh and serves as the foundation for the alimentary regimes adopted by the Orphics and Pythagoreans. Furthermore, the episode of the Titans highlights what we might call the figurative generative powers of the heart. The prohibition of the eating of animal flesh, understood by the Orphics and Pythagoreans to be an instance of cannibalism, finds its justification and grounding in the generative powers of the heart of the young god. What is most important for our purposes is the identification of the heart as the key term for a number of prohibitions and alimentary regulations that defined man's relation to his body and to the gods. To eat the heart amounts to eliminating any possibility of regeneration. For the heart is an organ with an outstanding intelligence, and as such it is the source and the principle of life.

The belief in the uniqueness of the status of the human heart is not limited to the Orphic and Pythagorean systems of belief. In fact, it extends to the Greek culture at large. In Aristotle's *De Motu Animalium,* we have perhaps the most accomplished version of the extension of the figurative powers of the heart. For Aristotle, the heart is not only the origin and center of life but also the guiding metaphor and analogy for the life and structure of the *polis* (city) itself: "It is clear that all animals have connate *pneuma* and derive their strength from this . . . This seems to bear a relation to the origin of life-activities that is similar to that which the point in the joints, the one which imparts movement and is moved, has to be unmoved. And since the origin is for some animals situated in the heart, for some in an analogous part, it is clear that the connate *pneuma* is also there . . . We should consider the organization of an animal to resemble that of a city well-governed by laws. For once order is established in a city, there is no need of a separate monarch to preside over every activity; each man does his own work as assigned, and one thing follows another because of habit."[2] Aristotle's heart provides the support and founding analogy for life in general, both biological and political.

The heart, the mechanical engine that animates the body and makes all movements possible, is also an archaic model for organization in general. It circulates, thanks to its centrality, between a number of orders and domains, between the biological and the mythological, the political and the physiological. From the narrative describing the death and rebirth of the young Dionysus to the biological texts locating the heart at the center of life, the heart fulfills the functions of centering and structuring theoretical discourses devoted to the analysis of a variety of manifestations of life in general. As such, the heart provides the basic conceptual tools in terms of which certain conceptions of life are articulated and organized. The heart is thus the guarantor of forms of exchange that make such discourses possible and intelligible.

An Impossible Mourning

My major concern in the texts that I will discuss in detail in this book will be the intersection of cannibalism and the heart. Furthermore, the act of cannibalism described in the majority of these texts follows a basic codified structure that exploits the symbolism of the social dimensions of the meal, the act of eating and sharing food together. In order to appreciate the full implications of this narrative deployment of the meal, it is necessary to discuss the anthropological and religious dimensions of the collective meal, its variations and different usages. In this perspective, the Titans' feasting on the dismembered body of Dionysus and its reception constitute one of the founding narratives that inform the development of the stories of the eaten heart. What are the basic elements at play in such perverse collective meals, and how do they relate to the more conventional acts of eating together?

Human societies define and characterize themselves to a large degree by what they eat and what they do not eat. Furthermore, the specific and distinct manner of preparing food constitutes a highly marked form of identification for any particular social group. Ritualized eating, in its many cultic and social manifestations, transcends the mere necessity of nourishment and establishes the meal (or any other gathering organized around food or eating) as a significant symbolic occasion demarcating communal boundaries and modes of identification and distinction. If the act of eating itself does not exhaust the symbolic potential of the meal, language, or, more precisely, communication plays a crucial role in the structuring of the eating ritual. The concept of the meal around the table is, so to speak, an institutionalized gathering that functions to set apart a space and a time where eating and speaking converge and intersect. The meal around the table recognizes that eating and speaking are two forms of expression and communication akin to each other, two separate languages that can come together and can be substituted for each other.

One case in which we can trace the exchange between food

and language is the funerary meal. In fact, one of the main functions of the funerary meal is not simply to remember the dead, but instead to be able to remember the dead as dead. In other words, the survivors who gather to share a meal after the burial of the dead identify their survival—that is, their crucial difference from the one who is dead—by eating together, by introducing food into their stomachs, whereas the dead person has been buried in the stomach of the earth. Thus, in this context, food, or the act of eating together, becomes a way of marking the difference between those who can eat and those who can no longer eat, between those who continue to eat together and those eaten by the earth.[3] The opposition between the two meals derives its functionality from the desire to separate the living and the dead. But what if the motivation behind such a meal—and this will be the case in the majority of our stories—is in fact to bring together the living and the dead under the guise and disguise of food? What if the driving force behind the meal is precisely the desire to abolish the possibility of mourning that is afforded the subject thanks to the funerary meal by veiling the death under the cover of food? In this case, we are forced to refine our description and analysis of "incorporation," of the different ways of introducing objects and words within the body.

In psychoanalytic terms, the "incorporation" we are concerned with here is best understood in terms of the opposition between introjection and incorporation and the manner in which they both try to provide the subject with ways of dealing with the experience of a loss, or the death of a loved one.[4]

Introjection, as its etymology indicates, means a throwing inside. In its technical sense, it denotes the impossibility of explicitly articulating and admitting a radical loss and the consequent inability to express through words the experience of this founding lack. The introjected language is therefore the negation of a fundamental lacuna experienced by the subject to the extent that it consists in the failed articulation of an experience located by the subject outside the possibility of figurative naming and representation. Introjection gives rise instead to a process of figuration through which a substitution, designed to allow a meaningful and intelligible discursive production, is accomplished by means of linguistic representations. In short, introjection allows the "normal" work of mourning to take place. But, in cases where such work is obstructed or suppressed, incorporation arises and substitutes for the normalizing effects of introjection. In other words, incorporation constitutes the limit and closure of introjection. The radical duality that grounds introjection, that is to say the failure to identify and to identify with the object of mourning, accounts for the illusory and artificial qualities of introjection and points to its secretive nature. The failure of introjection designates the work of incorporation as the production of a discursive proliferation that allows communication. In brief, incorporation transforms the dead and inoperative symbol into an active one. It makes it possible for the absent or dead person to speak and to be present. And therefore, it denies the necessity for mourning, since the dead are well and alive again.

This denial of loss occurs only up to a certain point, however, because the phantasm of incorporation is, in a strict sense, a private, almost a silent affair. It involves the subject and its imaginary representations of the survival of a lost object of love. Its generating motivation comes from the subject itself, from the subject's unwillingness to accept the effective loss or the disappearance of the desired object. The language activated by the phantasm of incorporation is thus a blind and a blinding one. This language is blind because it seeks to cover up the secret it carries from the subject itself in order to support and maintain the specificity and the autonomy of the incorporated object. It also is blinding because of its concerted efforts to camouflage its inherent weakness and constitutive fragility as well as the subject's suspicion of metaphors and of figurative discourse in general, a suspicion that gives place to a unique and often eloquent discourse that works to avoid the traps of figurality. The language of the secret, the language that is spoken from the position of the secret, constitutes itself as a secret language, and necessarily so. The unconscious effects of the act of incorporation transform the discourse of the subject into a private order of speech, bordering on silence, yet continuously haunted by the subject's fear of the nudity and the public exhibition of words. Such a discourse is ultimately an uncontrollable discourse because of the absolute and contradictory controls imposed on it that cause it to degenerate into a ritualized and highly coded "bavardage." Between the utopian silence and the actual words, the subject, irresistibly, traces an outline, a sketch of the foreign element that has invaded and transformed its most private space. The speaker, in the case of the phantasm of incorporation, thus utters words that are his words but that are also not his, words that ultimately belong to an other who cannot be recognized or named because it has, once and for all, disappeared, faded away under its own skin. The phantasm of incorporation unwillingly reiterates the loss it works so hard to negate and to deny. The funerary meal, on the other hand, because it is first and foremost a collective gathering, supports a structure that makes it possible to acknowledge and to accept, in the framework of a community defined and characterized by language and food as modalities of exchange and markers of boundaries, the death and the disappearance from this world of a member of that community. Whereas incorporation invites secrecy and forces the individual to withdraw from the community, the funerary meal publicizes the loss and identifies each individual as a member of a living group. The funerary meal thus functions as an effective preventive measure of anti-incorporation.

In this context, the stories of the eaten heart perform a curious inversion of the dynamics and the central structure of the funerary meal. They do so by exhibiting the effective power of a desire determined to put an end to the public display of the work of mourning, a desire that, in its founding effort, leads directly to a forced and secret incorporation, a literal incorporation that brings back with it the original structure negated by the work of mourning already in progress. The question raised by our disturbing tales appears to be, at first glance, quite simple: what happens when someone is secretly made to eat a part of the body of the person he or she loves? What happens, in other words, when the subject, instead of celebrating its survival and accepting its loss through a rehearsal of a version of the funerary meal, is made to eat the heart of the lover, dead and buried? The principal configuration deployed by these questions points to the intimate connections between the narrative organization of the tale and the function of the funerary meal as well as the severity of the displacement and the reorientation involved in this ritualized and conventional form of mourning in the story. Thus, in most of these narratives, the act of feeding the heart precedes and prepares the revelation of the death (and the murder) of the lover, and, consequently, the heart takes on a different significance. In these cases, the husband is the killer of the lover and the feeding of the heart is his ultimate revenge, a revenge that coincides with making his jealousy public as well as his retaliation to his wife's betrayal.

In all instances, however, the desire behind this kind of "forced incorporation" is a desire driven by a blind will to unleash a rehearsal of a real loss that has already taken place in order to articulate and to confirm its own status and position with respect to the detached and assimilated object. The motivation for this violent act of perverse projection stems from the subject's undeterred will to occupy, albeit under somewhat different circumstances, the same position as that of the dead lover, before and after his death. What grounds and supports the violence of this force-feeding is the effort to guide and control an operation of actual incorporation to which this all-powerful subject ultimately commits itself. This secret goal of the force-feeder requires an essentially doubly fictitious scenario that would allow its undetected emergence. The necessary fiction here relies on the figurative status of the heart and the accompanying apparatus that permits its double installation and transfer from the body to the sepulcher and then again to the body. The network of relations I am describing here turns around the interplay between the figurative and the literal, between the visible and the hidden, and the generalized figurative economy animating the symbolic investments of the body and its various representations in terms of food and speech. The body is the body of the dead lover, the body of the wife as wife and as lover of the dead; the body is also the body of the older texts, the corpus on which each tale operates. And it is precisely because of the overriding centrality of the tensions and conflicts underlying active figurative deployment, and the precise manner in which each narrative exploits this in the most simple and powerful terms, that each story is both the culmination of a long-established tradition and a new configuration of that tradition. In order to reveal this crucial and decisive relation to the tradition in its full implications, it is necessary to proceed with a careful and detailed analysis of the constitutive components of doubling and representation exploited in the narratives.

The phantasm of incorporation, as we have seen, depends on a secret and private referential system that evacuates, if not totally eliminates, the conventional referential structure informing figurative discourse. The funerary meal, on the other hand, institutes food and the specific conditions of assimilating it as the vehicle of a communal and collective code in terms of which both life and death may be represented in their crucial proximity and difference. The seventeenth-century tale "Le Coeur mangé" by Jean-Pierre Camus, for example, in its imposing relation to the narrative tradition of the eaten heart, tries, so to speak, to walk a fine line between these two poles, between the total and desperate abandonment of the figurative and the surrender to a generalized economy of referentiality. One way of tracking down the differences between incorporation and false incorporation and the accompanying operations involving a form of assimilation (of an other, of another text, and so forth) is to establish the modes of deployment of the enunciative positions of the participants or the agents in each scenario and the consequent distribution of responsibility and its representations. In the case of the phantasm of incorporation, the subject speaks the language of the other. It speaks, from the position of this other, a language designed to protect the secrecy of that which the subject itself cannot afford to acknowledge in its present condition. This first mode accounts to a large degree for Camus's relation to his sources, to texts that are difficult to come by and that are buried in now inaccessible books. For example, Camus's claim of making public certain texts in a revised form is a ruse and a fiction, as we shall shortly see, through which he effectively effaces the traces of what his text presents itself as the representative and representation. The funerary meal, on the other hand, makes possible a language that speaks the common bond between the survivors or the members of a community. Its language is a language of distantiation and separation in that it seeks to identify and to advertise the gap dividing the consumers of food and those consumed by the earth.

In Camus's "Le Coeur mangé," for instance, the eating of the dead lover's heart brings together the two conflicting dimensions represented by incorporation and the funerary meal. The body of the woman is both the secret hiding place of the organ standing for the missing lover and its final resting place. The intelligibility of this structure identifying the body of the woman with the sepulcher (and, as we shall see, the text of the tale itself) stems from its concentration on the modalities of the linguistic exchange in terms of which the agents of the narrative define themselves and establish their specificity. What informs and invests the act of substitution of the heart for food and love and/or jealousy is a certain disposition that privileges the heart as the central piece in the machinery of displacements and dislocations governing the overall organization of the narrative. Put differently, the heart rests at the intersection of the figurative and the literal, of the body and its passions, of food and speech. The heart functions like the principle and the life support mechanism of the peculiar figurative deployment necessary for the materialization of this perverse force-feeding. To return to our point of departure, the force-feeder occupies a position similar to that of the Titans. But instead of eating the human flesh himself, he makes his wife eat the disguised heart of her lover, and the regeneration of Dionysus is echoed, in our stories, by the death of the wife and her reunion with her dead lover.

The troubling question of cannibalism at the heart of the Dionysian myth has now been slightly displaced into a different context. The opposition between those who eat flesh and those who abstain from eating it is now replaced by that between those who are made to eat human flesh and those who consciously force them to do so. The sacrifice of Dionysus becomes, in our stories, the ambiguous and ambivalent substitute of the heart of the dead lover and all its conflicting connotations. We have moved from the world of the gods to the world of humans, dominated by jealousy and sexuality. We have moved from a world where the god's murder, sacrifice, and rebirth dictated some of the ways humans choose to live and to relate to each other and to the natural order by marking and distinguishing themselves by what they eat and what they refuse to eat, to the world of fiction and poetry where humans, mostly women, are secretly made to eat the flesh and heart of their dead and murdered lovers.

The Tale of the Two Brothers

Prior to the story of the murder and dismemberment of Dionysus at the hands of the Titans, there is an older story that combines the mythological dimension of the sacrifice of the young god with the tensions and conflicts occasioned by jealousy and sexual desire. The story, known as the "Tale of the Two Brothers," comes from ancient Egyptian literature.[5] The story is unique partly because it comes to us remarkably well preserved in the D'Orbiney Papyrus, and also because it presents us with a complex and subtle narrative that combines psychological and sociological description and analysis with a strong dose of mythological development. It is thus an excellent text for introducing us to the rich and violent universe of the heart and its cultural and cultic representations.

The tale begins as a simple narrative telling the story of conflict and envy between two brothers and then slowly moves on to the domain reserved for kings and gods. Along the way, it deploys a central cluster of modalities of representation focused on the heart that invoke sexuality, death, rebirth, and regeneration. The two brothers are initially nameless. They live together and work in the fields. One day the older brother's wife tries to seduce the younger brother, who rejects her sexual advances. She then proceeds to falsely accuse him of raping her, thus bringing conflict to the happy household. When the young man discovers that his older brother is trying to kill him, he decides to leave the household. The older brother chases the younger one until they come to a place where they are separated by water thanks to the intervention of the god Pre-Harakhti. The separation of the two brothers allows the young man to shout his version of the story to his older brother on the other side:

> Then the youth rebuked his elder brother, saying: "What is your coming after me to kill me wrongfully, without having listened to my words? For I am yet your young brother, and you are like a father to me, and your wife is like a mother to me. Is it not so that when I was sent to fetch seed for us your wife said to me: 'Come, let us spend an hour lying together'? But look, it has been turned about for you into another thing." Then he let him know all that had happened between him and his wife. And he swore by Pre-Harakhti, saying: "As to your coming to kill me wrongfully, you carried your spear on the testimony of a filthy whore!" Then he took a reed knife, cut off his phallus, and threw it into the water; and the catfish swallowed it. And he grew weak and became feeble. And his elder brother became very sick at heart and stood weeping for him loudly. . .
>
> Then his younger brother called to him, saying: ". . . I shall go to the Valley of the Pine. But what you shall do for me is to come and look after me, when you learn that something has happened to me. I shall take out my heart and place it on top of the blossom of the pine. If the pine is cut down and falls to the ground, you shall come to search for it." . . . Then he went to the Valley of the Pine; and his elder brother went to his home, his hand on his head and smeared with dirt. When he reached his house, he killed his wife, cast her to the dogs, and sat mourning for his younger brother. (206–207)

From the threat of incest to the full emergence of the mythological presence of the two gods Anubis (the older brother) and Bata (the younger brother), the "Tale of the Two Brothers" puts forward one of the most fundamental associations of sexuality and identity in the symbolic functions of the heart. Bata's self-castration, his ultimate gesture of loyalty to his elder brother, accompanies his exteriorization of his own heart as a full representative of himself, as a complete substitute for his identity and actions. The position of the heart directly reflects Bata's status and condition despite the fact that it has been severed from its body and organism. The central organ of the body, in its mythological dimension, retains its full powers as the principal indicator and representation of life. For in ancient Egypt, the heart lies at the center of life, emotions, and survival before and after death.[6] Furthermore, the heart, separated from its body, retains life and the power to maintain its intimate relations with the vital principle of the body. In other words, the heart is both a condensation of life as well as its ultimate metaphorical representation. It is both the sign and signature of life as well as its agency. Another interesting, and for our purposes highly significant, detail is the implicit relation between the heart and the phallus, between the heart as the organ that names life and and the phallus as the organ of male sexuality. Bata's self-castrating gesture accompanies and to a certain degree explains his separation from his heart, for the heart is already fully invested with the power to represent passion and its physical extension. This intimate intersection and intertwining of the vital principle of life with the sexual and emotional domains provide the fundamental structure underlying the different and at times opposing appropriations of the heart that we will encounter in later texts.

But Bata's story does not end with his separation from his vital organs. Anubis, the elder brother, spends three years looking for his younger brother:

> When it had dawned and the next day had come, and the pine had been felled, Anubis, the elder brother of Bata, entered his house. He sat down to wash his hands. He was given a jug of beer, and it fermented. He was given another of wine, and it turned bad. Then he took his staff and his sandals, as well as his clothes and his weapons, and he started to journey to the Valley of the Pine. He entered the mansion of his young brother and found his young brother lying dead on his bed. He wept when he saw his young

brother lying dead. He went to search for the heart of his young brother beneath the pine under which his young brother had slept in the evening. He spent three years searching for it without finding it. When he began the fourth year, his heart longed to return to Egypt, and he said: "I shall depart tomorrow." So he said in his heart. When it had dawned and another day had come, he went to walk under the pine and spent the day searching for it. When he turned back in the evening, he looked once again in search of it and he found a fruit. He came back with it, and it was the heart of his young brother! He fetched a bowl of cool water, placed it in it and sat down according to his daily custom. Then his heart stood in its place, and he became as he had been. Thereupon they embraced each other, and they talked to one another. (208–209)

Here again, the heart is the site not only of life but also of the regeneration and rebirth of the absent Bata. It is evident, in the context of the narrative, that the agricultural background, the general emphasis on the interaction between the land and water, partially explains the mythological valorization of the heart as the medium and agency of regeneration. Bata's revival is preceded by a curious moment in the text that brings communication, the discursive articulation of feelings and decisions, into and through the heart ("So he said in his heart"). It is as if the relations between the two brothers, since the initial conflict and the emergence of the heart as their means of communication, can now only take place in the heart. The two gods communicate with and relate to each other in and through their hearts. The inner thoughts of one bring back and revive the other thanks to his heart. What is here a purely mythological relation will become later on the grounds for friendship and its idealization.

The "Tale of the Two Brothers," one of the oldest literary documents we possess in which the heart plays a central role, displays and exploits all the functions and figurative variations of the heart that we will encounter in the following chapters: from the locus of communication to the site of the vital principle of life and regeneration to, ultimately, the place where passions, emotions, sexuality, and death come together. The heart is the organ and symbol of the most basic and yet crucial manifestations of life.

ONE

The Lure of the Heart

And just as we have died through appetite in Adam, so shall
we recover life through the taste of Christ, "as whence arose
death, thence shall life re-arise."

JACQUES DE VITRY, *DE SACRAMENTIS*

Never did a hen fall in love with a capon.

LITTRÉ, *DICTIONNAIRE*

In the Judeo-Christian tradition, the gesture that inaugurates the
Fall and the subsequent separation of man from God the Creator
is represented by the eating of the forbidden fruit of the tree of
knowledge. Man's expulsion from paradise, his discovery of his
limitations and of his status as man—in short, the founding
moment of human community—follows directly from the prohibited tasting of the apple and the transgression it represents.
In this exemplary instance, eating operates both as a form of
rupture and as a unifying bond. In fact, eating the apple functions
as an "eye-opener" in that it leads directly to the revelation of
the nudity and the fragility of the human body and inscribes the

Fall in terms of human mortality and sexuality.[1] Eating the forbidden fruit amounts to losing the protective shield provided by the Creator, a shield that is, in effect, a veil covering the body and its inherently tempting and dangerous seductions as well as its inadequacies. The loss of that veil presents the first man and woman with the spectacle of their nudity and sexual difference.

In the biblical narrative, eating and sexuality share a common ground at the origin, or, more specifically, through their mutual emergence and convergence they both mark an originary moment defined by separation and detachment from the origin itself. This initial encounter of sexuality and eating at the moment of creation and the Fall in the Bible played a major role in the determination and the elaboration of the theological discourse intended to address the question of sexuality. The taste of the apple thus initiates man into the order of sexuality and mortality, an order grounded in transgression and the consequent delimitation of the human domain as a rupture and a loss of the originary and the original.[2]

Christianity emphasizes the importance of this originary act of eating the apple by the unique and privileged role it reserves for the Eucharist and its redemptive powers. It is as if the only effective antidote to the negative and disastrous implications of the eating of the apple could come from another act of eating, the magical and mysterious eating of the body of Christ. Eating the apple represents a decisive separation and alienation from the divine order and the loss of the original state of creation. The Eucharist, in its full theological significance, recuperates the lost man and reintroduces him into the divine and originary body. Thus, in the Christian interpretation of the biblical narrative, eating the apple and the Eucharist represent two opposite yet complementary moments of rupture and reunion.[3] The Eucharist performs the (narrative) closure of the opening inaugurated by the first and decisive transgression, the first act of eating the forbidden fruit. The itinerary outlined by these two exemplary moments of assimilation and recuperation records the infinite distance separating the divine and the human body and their fundamentally different corporeality. But it also records a certain contamination, a form of inevitability and necessity that dictates a redoubling of the human transgression in the act intended to recover it and to neutralize it. This contamination reproduces, in a sense, the conditions of the original creation and consequently identifies the origin as a source of contagion or as a contaminating agency. The creation by mimesis calls for a mimetic recreation, a mimetic rebirth into the mystical body of Christ; it requires a repetition of the fall into sexuality and mortality in the form of a problematic duality of the closure of that fall.[4] This duality is most clearly highlighted by the peculiar and problematic form of "eating" that is the Eucharist, an invisible body that emerges as such through a magical metaphor and the powers of language.

This founding and exemplary narrative raises difficult and complex issues, and a full discussion would be beyond the scope of this chapter. I will turn now to some observations on the relations between eating, sexuality, and some models of exchange and substitution that support and display the allegorization of food and of the act of eating. I will begin with an interpretation of the *Lai d'Ignaure*, a thirteenth-century poem.[5]

The *Lai d'Ignaure* tells the tragic story of the life and death of a knight, Ignaure, and his love affairs. Ignaure, a resident at the castle of Riol, falls in love with the twelve married ladies who also live there with their husbands. One day, the ladies decide to play a game; they choose one among themselves to perform the role of the priest to whom all the rest will confess the name of their secret lover. One after another, the noble ladies name Ignaure as their lover. After the revelation of the identity of the unique secret lover, the ladies agree to avenge their love and plan a trap for Ignaure. They all consent to participate in what promises to be a cruel and gruesome revenge. The day finally arrives when Ignaure is caught in the trap, surrounded by twelve angry women armed with sharp knives. But instead of meeting his death, Ignaure, thanks to his beauty and intelligence, manages to take control of the situation. He first confesses his equal love for all the ladies, and then he is forced to choose one of them. Ignaure selects the lady who played the role of the priest and the one who proposed the solution to their dilemma. Not long after this, an informant discovers Ignaure's secret and tells the whole story to the husbands who, in their turn, decide to take their own revenge. One day they catch Ignaure with his chosen lady and put him away in a cell in the castle. After some deliberation, the husbands decide to feed their wives Ignaure's heart and penis. When the women are informed about Ignaure's fate and what they have done, they give up eating and die.

The *Lai d'Ignaure*, an early thirteenth-century text and one of the very first narratives of the legend of the eaten heart, displays a remarkable sophistication in its recapitulation of what one might call the figurative baggage or history of the heart. One important and highly revealing detail is the fact that the husband, in all the stories of the legend of the eaten heart, is never a cannibal. The husband is never tempted to consume the heart of his rival in a mad moment of rage and anger. The husband (or the agent I will call the force-feeder) understands all too well the requisites for maintaining the semblance of the possibility of a return or a recuperation of the transformed and disguised organs which he feeds his wife as his own, since he desires to see his own heart "eaten" by the love he so longs for. The force-feeder thus never joins in the meal, and if he does, he does not eat the heart of his rival. For anthropophagy is not the crucial issue for the husband. Cannibalism is always disguised, partly neutralized and naturalized by the simulation and the representational power of food and the culinary decorations and perfumes. In other words, the husband's assimilation of his rival is necessarily mediated, imaginary, and phantasmagoric. This assimilation reduces the body of the woman, the desired body and the body of an impossible and conflictual desire, to a mere playground, a hidden and interiorized screen on which the husband displays his absolute violence. The force-feeder seeks ultimately to introduce his own body into the body of the desired woman under the guise of the dead organs of the lover, and as the annihilation and absolute destruction of those organs. The double and paradoxical assimilation involving the husband and the dead lover overdetermines the heart and the phallus and extracts their power of representation from a specific literary and cultural tradition. This text also defines a relatively new problematic for its staging of the narrative in the way in which it recuperates and distances itself from a number of earlier texts whose primary objective appears to be the representation of the heart as the central element in a cultic or ritual configuration. Thus, it seems appropriate at this point to discuss briefly the Dionysian configuration of the heart and some of its culinary implications.

Cor ne edito (Eat not the heart): Pythagoras' absolute prohibition lies at the center of a number of cultural representations that, at least up until the major neoplatonists, named and defined the heart as the locus and paradigmatic organ embodying the intellectual foundation for dietary, cultic, and religious practices. It also identifies a violent and sacrificial narrative at the origin of those practices and representations. The story is well known but also worth retelling. The Titans, the first creatures of the Earth, kidnap the child Dionysus. Before they can sacrifice the young god, they have to get him to produce a visible sign of consent, a necessary gesture in the Greek sacrificial code. They give him food and toys, but to no avail. Finally, they hand him a fogged mirror.[6] Unable to recognize himself in the vague and distorted reflection produced by the mirror, he nods his head in a vain search for his own image and identity. This quest, in its telling motions and gestures, is interpreted by the Titans as his consent to be sacrificed. They kill and dismember Dionysus; then they proceed to boil and broil his flesh, after which they feast. But before they can consume his heart, Athena informs Zeus of their sacrilege, and he destroys the Titans with lightning and returns them to the Earth. The god is regenerated and reborn from his uneaten heart.[7]

This central episode in the Orphic and Pythagorean Dionysian corpus links violent death, sacrifice, dismemberment, and rebirth to misrecognition and loss of identity and the consequent diversity and multiplicity that such a loss produces. It locates the emergence and confirmation of identity with a prior state of loss or confusion and distortion and the ensuing necessary fragmentation and dispersal of the body. Between the dismembered body and the identity inhabiting it, the ties are reinforced by the violence. Indeed, it seems that at least in the case of Dionysus, the constituent identity is generated by the violent dismemberment of the body. For the heart is the organ with an outstanding intelligence, and as such it is the principal source of life. According to Philo of Alexandria, the heart "takes shape before the rest of the body, just like the foundation of a house or the keep of a ship. And they say that the heart still palpitates after death so that it disappears last just as it appears first."[8] For the Pythagoreans, the privileged status of the heart, especially in its function as the origin and the organizer of human life, brings out its intimate relations to sperm, the other principal source of human life.[9] According to Detienne, sperm is thought of in precisely the same terms as the heart. What is most important for our purposes is the identification of the heart as the key term for a number of prohibitions and alimentary regulations that defined man's relation to his body and to the gods. Dionysus' heart, in its symbolic survival and regenerative powers, becomes the paradigmatic representation of an originary moment where life and death, sacrifice and murder, anthropophagy and food, all converge. The heart that is not eaten by the Titans, the heart that survives the savage murder of a god, becomes the object of the prohibition intended to avoid the act it symbolizes by its sheer presence.

This brief excursion into the culinary and sacrificial dimension of the heart in Greek cultic and cultural thought illustrates the centrality as well as the specificity of the heart as the locus of a number of pregnant investments demarcated by prohibition. The heart, the origin and support system of life, is also the principal generator of a chain of metaphors and figures that inscribe it as a limit and as an end in itself. The central organ of the body, in its representation and through its representational powers, becomes the central operative principle of figurative discourse, of a textual corpus.

The Woman, the Heart, and the Phallus

The emergence of the heart and the phallus in a text like the *Lai d'Ignaure* "incorporates" the narrative itself; it makes a body with its own central organ. Indeed, the *Lai d'Ignaure* deploys both an incorporation and the constitution or formation of a related body. In order to grasp this incorporation and to demarcate this body, this corpus, we have to follow the logic of dismemberment put into place in the poem.

The genesis of dismemberment describes the gradual and fatal emergence of the loss of multiplicity and plurality, a loss that is, at the end of the poem, doubly inscribed. The first confession naming a single lover corresponds to Ignaure's forced confession when he must choose a single lady. The poem names this reduction, this loss, as the direct source for Ignaure's death: "A mouse with a single hole cannot live long . . . The mouse with only one hole / is quickly taken and trapped" (373, 480–481). On the

{25}

other hand, the husbands' feast during which their wives' betrayal is revealed corresponds to the confession scene during which Ignaure's betrayal is revealed to the ladies. It is as if, in the logic of the poem, the confessional setting corresponds to the setting of the meal—as if confessional discourse corresponds to and is the equivalent of food. Food and words articulate, each in its own register, the exchanges and the substitutions that constitute the story of Ignaure, and at the center of this story lies the identification or the secret naming of the body of the woman as the sepulcher. The woman's body is the resting place but also the place of transgression. The deposition of the heart and the phallus, disguised as food, into the woman's body rehearses and puts an end to the initial transgression and designates the body as the locus for exchange and reciprocity. And the last scene of the poem, the scene of the secret feeding of the dismembered Ignaure to his lovers, is a double scene: it is first a scene of secret and forced incorporation, and, second, a funerary meal, a celebration of the death of the rival. In the space between the two, the *Lai d'Ignaure* animates a curious exchange between incorporation and mourning, between eating and sexuality. Such an exchange takes place, in the poem, in the framework of a ritualized parody of the Last Supper, a transgression and perversion of an established and founding narrative. The *Lai d'Ignaure* tells its story on the margins of sacramental theology and the intersection between Christian and Greek mythology. And it is precisely in this context and against this background that the transgression of the *Lai* becomes most significant.

The basic structure of the *Lai d'Ignaure* thus puts into play all the necessary elements for the formation of a phantasm of incorporation.[10] And yet it is evident that mourning, or at least a first stage of mourning, takes place in the poem and that this initial, public mourning leads, through the perverse situation described in the text, to a form of "literal" and primitive incorporation, namely, the feeding of the penis and the heart.[11] From the point of view of a theory of cryptonomy, the incorporation described in the text is a false or "artificial" incorporation because it is motivated from the outside, desired and initiated by another subject whose principal aim appears to be the ending of a public display of mourning. The driving motivation behind the husbands' action is their effort to operate a fundamental substitution, a transfer between the inside and the outside that could ultimately cover up what was most publicized. Thus, the *Lai d'Ignaure* allows us to look into a peculiar situation exhibiting the genesis and the structure of a phantasm of incorporation without its customary secrecy and hidden machinations. The *Lai* narrates an instance of reversed or inverted incorporation. But this "incorporation" is not limited to the level of the narrative; it also affects the whole poem.

The husbands' action mimics the formation of a phantasm of incorporation, but it does so only up to a point because this phantasm is, in a strict sense, a private, almost silent affair. It involves the subject and its imaginary representations of the survival of a lost object of love. Its generating motivation comes from the subject itself, from its unwillingness to accept the effective loss or the disappearance of the desired object. The phantasm of incorporation emerges from a part of the subject that is unknown, unrevealed, and undiscovered. Or, put differently, the phantasm of incorporation invents this secret part of the subject, this unknown subject, in order to accommodate and to host the magical survival of the lost object. In order for the crypt to occupy a space clearly marked for it, that is, in order for it to constitute itself as such, there must exist an absolutely other part of oneself where it may come and rest. Or rather the crypt, by its sheer presence, transforms itself into the space it invades and thus inhabits it as if it were already a secret, other, or inaccessible part of the subject. The crypt brings with it the irreversible transformation and transfiguration of the structure of the host it penetrates for the sake of its survival and autonomy.

The phantasm of incorporation is thus characterized primarily by its secrecy, by its tendency to develop elaborate deceptions to protect the subject from the inherent dangers of the secret it retains inside as well as the secrecy of the thing that has introduced itself surreptitiously and silently into the innermost part of the subject. The refusal to accept or even to admit the real or potential loss of the loved object and the subsequent animation of the dead object in and as a crypt require a detachment from the public and collective space and a withdrawal from the common language. In the *Lai d'Ignaure* this withdrawal and detachment are signified by food, by the refusal to eat and the consequent identification between eating and a form of knowledge. The silence of the husbands concerning Ignaure's fate is echoed by the fasting of the ladies. The empty mouth corresponds to the silent mouth. The husbands' solution or answer to the challenge is most significant and revealing:

> One says: "These ignoble debauched ones
> Have all sworn to fast
> Until the moment when it will be known
> Whether he will die or live.
> In four days we will take
> From him precisely this fifth member
> That gave them so much pleasure.
> We will make a meal out of it for them.
> We will add to it his heart.
> We will make twelve servings out of it,
> By ruse we will have them eat it.
> For we cannot better avenge ourselves!"
> The plan was approved:
> They dismembered the good knight.
> (537–550)

The husbands' ruse, their ultimate revenge, consists in feeding the dismembered desired body to their wives. This perverse undertaking appears to have a double function. First, it serves as a form of protection against incorporation, against the ultimate betrayal dreaded by the husbands. It does so because it is performed and enacted by the husbands as a form of a funerary meal. The collective aspect of the funerary meal, its introduction of food as a ritualized sign of the departure of the deceased into the other world, the clear separation it institutes between the living, assembled together, and the dead, unseen and buried in the ground—all these features work to highlight the crucial difference between the dead and those who can join together and share a meal. The funerary meal, by making it possible to consume food collectively in a relatively public space, to introduce food into the bodies of the participants as if to avoid the threat of introducing the body of the dead instead, transforms the act of eating into a form of collective and communal language that publicly declares the death of the dead and the survival of the living. The collective nature of the meal therefore acknowledges the uninterrupted communication among the living and, in a sense, celebrates survival as a function of this language that is shared by the concerned community. It celebrates survival and death in terms of communication and is a model of exchange between food and language, between the living on the one hand and the dead on the other. The husbands' first action exploits these characteristics of the funerary meal but only in order to pervert them, in order to displace them into a second register.

This second register relies on a network of relations and relays in terms of which the murder of the lover is displaced and circulated as a condensation, one that is made possible, in the logic of the poem, by the shift from multiplicity to univocity. The condensation in question here brings back the plurality because it necessitates the repetition of the act of feeding. Thus, in the place of the dangers of the secret act of incorporation we have, in the *Lai d'Ignaure*, something like a forced incorporation that occurs only after the fact, after any real possibility of incorporation in the strict, technical sense of the term. The actual and material consumption of the other or of a privileged part of the other is now necessarily surreptitious, initiated from the outside, activated and enforced from a position of power and control, from the peculiar perspective of a subject desiring either to set in motion anew the work of mourning or to put an end to the mourning already begun. In both instances, the desire behind what I am calling here a forced incorporation is a desire driven by a blind will to unleash a rehearsal of a real loss that has already taken place in order to articulate and to confirm its own status and position with respect to the detached and assimilated object. The motivation for this violent act of projection stems from the subject's (that is, the husband's) will to occupy, albeit under somewhat different circumstances, the same position as that of the dead lover, before and after his death. What grounds and supports the violence of this forced feeding is an effort to control an operation of actual incorporation to which this all-powerful subject ultimately commits itself.

After the act of feeding Ignaure's organs disguised as food comes the moment of the revelation of truth, the moment of naming the transgression:

> When their heart had come back to them,
> Each one begged her lord
> For the love of God, to tell them if [Ignaure]
> Was out of jail.
> The one who seized him in his house
> Replied: "My lady who played the priestess,
> You were already his mistress.
> You have eaten what you greatly desired,
> What pleased you so much

That you desired nothing else.
In the end you were well served!
I killed and destroyed your lover:
All of you participated in the pleasure
That women desire so much;
Have you had enough, the twelve of you?
We are thoroughly avenged of our shame!"
(560–575)

The wives speak only after they have eaten the heart of their lover, only after they have literally regained their own heart ("When their heart had come back to them"). The husbands' response speaks the language of distantiation and separation in that it seeks to identify and to advertise the gap dividing the consumers of food and those who are consumed and literally were forced to consume the object of their passion. In the scenario of forced feeding, the speaker, the ultimate *metteur en scène,* utters the words that name his rival and that, in the same gesture, aim at ending this rivalry and establishing a new order. The words of the husband in this instance inaugurate a new pattern of relations between food and language, between the living and the dead, between the inside and the outside, between the figurative and the literal. The speaker who in this case is always a betrayed lover cannot but speak, if only for one single moment, the language of the other, the language of the desire of the dead. He cannot but name that dead as if he were still alive, acting through his name and the powers of his organs. He cannot but recall, one last time, what his actions have tried to conceal and dissolve under the disguise of an exchange between the body and food, an exchange that can only materialize inside another body, the body of the woman. In his mad act of revenge, the husband is ultimately betrayed by his own ruse, by his inevitable reliance on a model of exchange that requires the forbidden and unwanted

{31}

union between the wife and the dead lover. Thus, instead of a strict linear model of identification between food and speech, the forced-feeding scenario institutes a second and more complex model, a model of a second order.

This secondary form of identification draws on the models I have located in the case of the phantasm of incorporation and that of the funerary meal. On the one hand, the husband initiates a disguised request through the surreptitious introduction of his rival in his most significant representation into the body of the woman, an introduction that constitutes itself as an act of introjection in the etymological sense of the word. In the same gesture, the husband prefigures the return of the predictable answer to his demand for reciprocity thanks to a complex simulation, an intricate ruse that rehearses, before the act, the effects of that return. In other words, eating, or, more precisely, force-feeding and speaking, cooperate in establishing what is in fact an impossible communion, an impossible and forbidden union. This perverse union of the two bodies constitutes a transgression of the normal forms of exchange, since under the actual circumstances no transfer of "goods" is feasible. What remains, what both sender and receiver are left with, is simply a moment of recognition, an instance of linguistic naming and representation that is supported by the power of language and its capacity to bring about a reincarnation of the dead, of the dead body inside the body of its lover. This reincarnation takes the form of a dismembered discourse, a fragmentary recollection of the dead lover:

> While they were still alive they mourned aloud:
> One mourned his beauty,
> Such handsome and well-shaped limbs
> That the most handsome in the world were ugly beside them;
> Thus spoke two ladies.
> Another mourned his great courage,

And his graceful body and his generosity;
And the fourth, his eyes, his flanks,
That were so alive and so joyous.
(588–596)

The multiple and fragmented invocations of the dead lover derive from a structure consisting of a series of deferrals syncopated by motivated linguistic interventions through which filters out a name, or a set of names, designating a fundamental loss and an irredeemable absence, a name that redoubles and in a sense negates that loss and absence. The word that surfaces to designate and to identify the new location and the new face of the deformed element interiorized inside the body of the woman is a word that reiterates, by its sheer power of presence and "presentification," what has already taken place. The emergence, for example, of the name of the dead lover, an emergence that names his double death and survival, relates the end of the narrative of love and the ending that interrupted and halted the model of exchange and substitution that had made it possible.[12] The name of the dead that comes to confirm the new death of what it designates retraces in a single gesture the genesis of a frustrated desire of separation and irreversible discontinuity in the narrative in the manner in which it simulates a shift of responsibility, a declaration of loss, a missed opportunity. The name of the disguised and dead lover haunts the speaker. The force-feeder is also haunted by the inescapable irony of the return and the survival of something that exists no more except in representation and as a representation. This representation, however, can only survive inside a body, in the sepulcher or under the skin of the desired other, disguised and hidden from all. And this survival which, as in the case of a phantasm of incorporation, will ultimately lead to the destruction of the subject in its effort to protect that which it has incorporated, calls for a complete withdrawal from all that can contaminate the new seat and hiding place of the object. Hence the wives' decision to abstain from food, a decision that is presented in the poem as both a form of revenge and an affirmation of the incomparable quality of what they were secretly fed, and therefore of something that must be protected against any contamination or pollution:

> They swore an oath to God:
> That they would never eat again,
> Unless they were offered such a precious dish.
> (584–586)
> . . .
> "Alas! We have changed you so much;
> Their vengeance was too cruel.
> The jealous [husbands]! But we will not eat:
> And thus will we avenge ourselves."
> (599–602)

The women's decision to defend and protect the purity of their dead lover culminates in their deaths. Their revenge thus takes the form of a departure from this world with their lover. And after their deaths, the poet goes on to tell us:

> The elegy of the twelve of them was made,
> In a lay of twelve lines
> That one should remember well,
> Because the contents is completely true.
> (617–620)

The dismemberment of the lover and the distribution of his combined organs to his lovers give rise to the poem in a manner that clearly identifies both the lovers and the sexual organ and heart with the vehicle for poetic signification. Ignaure's dismemberment corresponds to the division of the initial poem, and thus the desired body and the poetic corpus echo each other in a text that displays the transgression of sexuality in terms of food and eating in order to name the dynamics of transgressive desire as the motor of poetic expression. The transgression in question here becomes evident when one compares the *Lai d'Ignaure* with the *Roman du châtelain de Couci et de la dame de Fayel* or with the stories of the eaten heart in the *Decameron*. In the *Roman du châtelain de Couci,* for instance, the husband is not responsible for the death of the lover, nor is he responsible for his dismemberment. Instead, it is the lover himself who, just before his death, decides to send his heart to his lady as a last gesture of love and devotion. The husband merely intercepts the "package" and feeds the heart secretly to his wife. This does not account, however, for the important difference between the two texts. The difference lies, I believe, in the specific manner in which the *Lai d'Ignaure* thematizes its poetic transgression through its uncanny features.[13] The strangeness of the *Lai* derives from its brutality, from its unparalleled violence in the legend of the eaten heart. And yet this violence and brutality are articulated in a clear and somewhat facile parody of the Christian founding narrative. The constitution of the Christian community, the founding of the *ecclesia,* is displaced here and subverted into a narrative describing the founding of a community defined by its dynamics of desire, a community of women devoted to the memory of a single lover. This community, a poetic community par excellence since poetic expression is a function of sexual desire in terms of the poem itself, dedicates itself to the memory of a transgression in the name of which the established order is destabilized and questioned.

Furthermore, the gender displacement operating in the text, along with the feeding of the combined and disguised phallus and heart, indicates a conscious separation between the heart and the penis on the one hand, and an intact body on the other, with a clear celebration of the body as it is represented by its most essential and desirable organs. The *Lai* celebrates the imprisonment of the organs inside the body of the lover and their impossible and perverse union. It also celebrates the imprisonment of the dead lover as a lover who dies for his desire and for whose love the twelve ladies sacrifice themselves. Along these lines, one is tempted to read into the parody of the Christian narrative of the Last Supper a Dionysian infiltration or interference that recalls the dismemberment of the god and evokes his rebirth and regeneration as well as his special powers and roles with women.[14] What is Dionysian about the narrative is precisely the violence of the husbands, the violence that comes to interrupt and interfere with the free reign of desire. For in the *Roman du châtelain de Couci,* as we shall see, the lover himself sends his heart to his lady. Here, the decision to feed Ignaure's organs to his lovers comes from the husbands and is motivated by jealousy and a blind drive to avenge the wives' adultery.

In its celebration of sexual desire through dismemberment, the *Lai d'Ignaure* appears to be motivated by an effort to rehabilitate something that was demystified by the Christian tradition, something that was lost in the domination of an ethical discourse privileging soul over body. This rehabilitation constitutes perhaps the secret of the *Lai,* its hidden desire, a desire that seeks to uncover a body in order to substitute for it another missing and powerful body, a unique and secret body. I began this chapter with a discussion of two exemplary narratives and two corresponding structures of mourning. Both practices, each in its own way, constitute specific modes of relating to the loss of a loved person or an object of love. In both instances the loss is generally perceived to represent a potential or ultimate threat to the fate of the subject or the community. The funerary meal presents us with a closed structure, a circular structure organized as an analogical network of relations and substitutions that permit a community to neutralize and overcome the loss of one of its members through an identification and exchange between language and food. On the other hand, the phantasm of incorporation, because of its secrecy, constitutes an open-ended structure, a hermeneutic structure devoted to nostalgia and the effective negation of mourning through the repudiation of its conditions of possibility. The phantasm of incorporation forms a secret structure designed to maintain and protect an inadmissible secret. The *Lai d'Ignaure,* in the way it parodies, recapitulates, and reorients a narrative around a theological tradition, activates and puts into place a powerful closure of "traditional" and courtly answers to the Christian model, answers we will find in Boccaccio's *Decameron* and the *Roman du châtelain de Couci.* At the same time, and with the same gesture, it puts forward death and its symbolic reanimation and reincarnation as a paradigm for poetic expression of a structure of signification grounded in the dynamics of desire. This reinscription of the poetic structure in terms of desire negates the Christian narrative parodied in the *Lai* and names its quest as that of a lost body, a dismembered body that provides and guarantees coherence and meaning.[15]

The theological narrative parodied in the *Lai d'Ignaure* is founded on a radical loss, the loss of the body of Christ. The phantasmagoric structure initiated by the husbands is overpowering because it rehearses and displaces an unnamed mystery, the Eucharist, that is to say, Christianity's magical metaphor of food and wine becoming body and blood. And the Eucharist, instead of being an act of incorporation of the dead and the missing, constitutes itself as the moment and modality of incorporating the living body into a larger body, into the symbolic body of the dead and resurrected. This other incorporation celebrates rebirth and resurrection of and through a new corpus, the Church. The poem denies and negates the mystery by its strong and clear parody as well as its insistence on the necessity to name the mystery:

> Meaning is lost if it is hidden;
> What is shown and discovered
> Can germinate anyplace.
> (11–13)

The transgression in the poem lies precisely in the secret feeding of Ignaure's organs to his lovers. And the transgression that the poem itself performs stems from its declared and uninhibited celebration of dismemberment and parody as vehicles for poetic signification.

   The *Lai d'Ignaure,* as we have seen, tells its tragic story in the confined space of a castle inhabited by twelve knights and their ladies. When the knights achieve their revenge, secretly feeding Ignaure's heart and phallus to their ladies, they are reproducing, in the poem's final scene, a communal meal closely resembling the feast of the Titans. The ladies, however, consume only the heart and the sexual organ of their lover and not his body disguised as food. This inversion is central to all the narratives of the legend of the eaten heart. Furthermore, this last scene mimics and parodies another great founding scene of eating, the Last Supper. The revelation of Ignaure's seduction of the ladies starts with an innocent game in which one of them is chosen to play the role of a priest to whom all the others will confess their secret love affair with Ignaure. Thus, the parody of the Last Supper is doubly inscribed in the narrative, first through the exploitation of the simulation of confession and second because this is the last meal of the ladies. But in this instance, it is twelve ladies who feast on the desired organs of the body of their lover. Although the offering is secret and disguised, it nevertheless reproduces a literal, physical union between the ladies and their dead lover. The *Hoc est corpus meum* becomes the literal offering of an other under the guise and the disguise of food.

The Husband as Eternal Rival and Voyeur

The *Roman du châtelain de Couci et de la dame de Fayel* (from
the late thirteenth century) tells its story across distant geographical boundaries, between the Holy Land and the home of the
Lady of Fayel.[16] The geographical distance is crucial here because
it highlights and puts into place the guiding organizing structure
of the text, establishing an economy of exchange and a network
of circularity and reciprocity that drive the narrative and invest
the various representations of bodily parts and organs. The Lady
of Fayel cuts off her braids and gives them to her lover as a sign
of her love prior to his departure for the Holy Land. Her detached braids are not only a mark of her love, they are literally
her heart: "If you love me as much as you say, you will take them
with you, and with them my heart will accompany you, and if
without killing myself I could tear it out, I would give it to you!"
(241). The conditional original gift specifies the operative representations through which the narrative will proceed and sets up
the modalities of substitution and displacement active in the
exchange between the two lovers. The cutting off of the braids
represents, at this stage of the narrative, the impossible but
desired wound, the opening of the body and the centrality of the
literal status of the heart. In fact, it is the drive toward the
literalization of this initial exchange and the fulfillment of its
haunting nostalgia that best describes the unfolding of the narrative.

The châtelain is mortally wounded by a poisoned arrow, and
before his death he dictates a letter to his lady and entrusts his
servant, Gobert, to deliver the letter with a silver box containing
her braids and his heart. The letter accompanying the heart spells
out and confirms the terms of the exchange, of what we might
term the contract of love and its tragic representations, between

the châtelain and his lady: "And because I know, because I am sure that I took your heart with me when I left Fayel and you gave me the jewel, so beautiful and gracious, that are your noble and brilliant braids which I have kept to this hour; I now send you my heart: it is right that you should possess it" (243). In return for the braids, the figurative representatives of the heart, the châtelain sends back his heart, thus fulfilling his lover's wishes and desires. And it is precisely the geographical distance that makes possible the literalization of the initial figurative status of the heart. Absence and distance, instead of deepening the powers of representation, lead to its annihilation, to its absolute and irreversible materialization. Furthermore, they open up the space for other exchanges and substitutions, since they require an emissary and an intermediary. These new and uncontrolled substitutions will work to undo and undermine the powers implied and embodied by the heart of the dead châtelain by introducing violence into the strict economy of exchange between the two lovers.

Gobert returns to Fayel and is discovered by the lady's husband, who interrogates him about the purpose of his visit and the contents of the package he is carrying. Gobert promises to reveal his secret mission to the husband and assures him of the death of the châtelain on the condition that the husband spare his life. His words are revealing because they indicate his awareness of the impending potential violence: "Dear lord, I beg you to have pity on me and to listen to me for an instant; I will tell you the whole story from end to end, but on the condition that you do me no harm, that you touch not one of my limbs and that you not take away my life!" (247). The husband then proceeds to force open the silver box, where he discovers his wife's braids and the accompanying heart and letter. He takes the heart and orders his cook to prepare it and to serve it only to the lady at a special meal: "The lord spoke to his chef and strictly ordered him to do everything in his power to prepare a dish of hens and capons so good that no one would want to change anything about it: —You will serve this dish, in particular, to all those who will be in the great hall, and you will make another dish out of this heart that you will serve to the mistress and to no one but her" (248).

The structure of the meal organized by the husband to celebrate his revenge and triumph over his dead lover combines the communal supper with the exclusion of the wife. She is present at the table but eats a separate course, one especially designed for her. The meal scene in the *Roman du châtelain de Couci* echoes the communal meal of the Titans and the one in the *Lai d'Ignaure,* but with a determining difference. The lady is singled out; she is set aside and almost separated and excluded from the social dimension implied by the communal meal. Her food identifies her as the outsider and the disloyal wife. Furthermore, her meal, after the revelation of its content, is seen to have a unique nature. On the one hand, it becomes literally a last supper since the lady will refuse to eat anything after her last reunion with the heart of her dead lover: "In the name of God, my lord, I am distraught because of this, and as it is so, I promise you with all certitude that I will never again eat and that I will not take a single mouthful of another food. My life is too heavy to carry! Death, deliver me from my life!" (250). This last supper brings together in a single moment two paradoxical dimensions. On the one hand, the lady eats what rightfully belongs to her—what is, in terms of the narrative, literally hers, that is to say the heart that is not only her lover's but also hers. In other words, the last supper, in this instance, is also an act of autophagy and as such echoes the Christian last supper. Her husband seems to understand that only she can eat what she eats, because of the figurative structure of the meal. On the other hand, the lady's last supper functions as a funerary meal for her dead lover. While the other guests and her husband are enjoying a meal traditionally served for Christmas, she eats the last material memory of her lover. Her literal introjection or interiorization of the heart signals the closure of the economy of exchange established at the opening of the *Roman* and returns the heart, forced out of its silver box, to its proper and only appropriate container. Between these two meals, between what is offered and disguised as food and what is really eaten, lies the distance separating the husband's desires and his wife's unintended satisfaction.

It is important to note here that in all the stories of the legend of the eaten heart, at least to my knowledge, the husband never partakes of his rival's heart. In fact, it seems that the heart of the dead lover is perceived as a taboo for all except the lady. Furthermore, in all the versions of the legend the wife is made to eat her lover's heart secretly, in disguise, and only after she has consumed it is she informed of what she has really eaten. This detail is highly significant, for it emphasizes the secret motivations of the husband, his double motivation. On the one hand, he desires to put an end to the love affair between his wife and her lover through the closure of the possibility of their physical union. His gesture, however, reproduces a last union between the two, between their two hearts. On the other hand, he desires to occupy the position of his dead rival, to be the one desired and loved by his wife. His secret feeding of the heart, in this instance, turns the last supper into a voyeuristic scene in which he observes the union of the two lovers and perceives himself in the position of power and authority. His gesture inevitably unleashes a sequence of events leading to the death of the wife and the confirmation of her dedication to her dead lover. It is as if by violently forcing his wife to eat her lover's heart and publicly mourn his death, the husband surreptitiously separates himself from the scene and becomes simply a helpless observer and spectator. The scene he initiates signals his own irrevocable exclusion from his relationship to his wife. His revenge is double-edged and results in the loss of his desired object. His feast celebrating the disappearance of his rival and his forced interiorization by the wife turns into his own last meal with his wife.

The voyeuristic dimension of the husband's actions confirms his status as the real outsider and the one excluded from the exchanges between the two lovers. As such, he fails to grasp the full implications of the modalities of representation instituted by the two lovers. His revenge and its ultimate failure result from his inability to perceive the powers of the literalization inaugurated by the two lovers at the moment of their separation. The literal value of the heart is temporarily lost because of the necessity of mediation, because of the violent and uninformed intervention of the husband. His disguising of the heart as human food, however, reactivates the discursive and representational contract between the two lovers. It is as if the double figuration of the heart as both food and the site and locus of passions returns it to its original simplicity and literality, to its original transparency. The legend of the eaten heart tells its story between these two registers, between what is prepared as food and what is eaten, between what is represented by the food eaten and the act of eating itself. The orality of the last supper reinvokes and reactivates the verbal contract between the lady and her dead lover and neutralizes the violence and jealousy of the husband. In the end, it confirms his status as the absolute outsider and the eternal rival.

The husband's predestination to the position of the rival is inscribed, in the *Roman,* in terms of his own fate. After the death of his wife, he is overtaken by remorse and buries her with great honors. But "it took very little time before her parents learned of it and accused him of having killed her for no reason by making her eat the heart of her lover. They wished to exact vengeance. Why say more? The lord of Fayel was reconciled to them by agreeing to leave the country and go overseas. He didn't stay there very long, and came back" (251). The revenge exacted by the parents forces the husband to repeat the lover's gesture, his separation from his lady. His travels, so to speak, complete his education. He returns to die, but only after having fully understood the pains of separation and the perversity of his actions. His remorse simply fulfills the words of his rival in naming his lady as an exemplary model of perfection: "You are a model worthy to direct all the ignorant in the path of wisdom, honor and dignity" (251). The husband's fate, his tragic destiny, stems from his ignorance: ignorance of the meaning of a lover's contract, of his wife's powers, and of his own desires. His fate is best symbolized by the structure of the meal he orders for himself and his guests, a feast of "hens and capons." He tries to bring together the two elements that can no longer come together, because of a radical difference and absence; and he, in his ignorance, is none other than the "capon." Between husband and wife, sexual desire is no longer possible. The relation between the wife and her lover, enforced and strengthened by the forms of exchange instituted by them to represent sexual desire despite their physical separation, excludes, once and for all, the husband from any possibility of sexual possession of his wife. The meal he prepares for his wife, her last supper designed to punish her and to exclude her, will also, thanks to that which is offered as food to both the wife and the rest of those present, symbolically exclude the husband from the scene of desire. The husband is no longer desirable, for "never did hen fall in love with a capon."

The rehabilitation of the lady at the conclusion of the narrative is not simply a manifestation of the conventional valorization of the feminine figure in the story; it is also a direct consequence of the internal structure of the tale and its economy of exchange and representation centered around the heart and the interplay between the figurative and the literal. The lady and her lover constitute a community founded on love and explicit, discursive exchange. The husband, necessarily excluded from this community, fails to situate himself in the position he desires. His failure merely reproduces his ignorance and his inability to channel his desires through discourse; it results from his trickery and violence and the violation of the discursive contract that was in place.

The *Roman du châtelain de Couci et de la Dame de Fayel* and the *Lai d'Ignaure* set forth the initial terms through which the legend of the eaten heart will be developed and deployed. Their complex and sophisticated exploitation of the legend makes them the paradigmatic texts that inform all the later explorations of the narrative of the eaten heart. From the enclosed space of the castle to the apparently infinite distance separating the Holy Land from France, the two narratives inscribe their tales of ritual murder and sacrifice, of the conflict between the desired but absent or inaccessible body and the desire for absolute possession of the heart of the dead lover and its generative symbolic powers. The heart, the symptom and locus of life, becomes the agent of figuration and disfiguration of the powers and horrors of love. In both narratives, the journey of the heart follows the same path, from the body of the lover to the body or bodies of the ladies and finally to the sepulcher. It is this trajectory, but with a crucial and significant deflection, that we now have to follow.

TWO

"Vide Cor Tuum"

And often I have asked myself whether, taking a large view,
philosophy has not been merely an interpretation of the body
and a misinterpretation of the body.

NIETZSCHE, *THE GAY SCIENCE*

In the *Roman du châtelain de Couci* the heart functions as the
central operator of identification and recognition between the
lady, her husband, and the dead lover. The underlying support
for this identification rests on the valorization of the heart as the
only viable substitute for sexuality. Indeed, this relation between
the heart and sexuality is overdetermined in the case of the *Lai
d'Ignaure*, because, as we have seen, the heart is served along
with the phallus to the twelve ladies. In both cases, the intercon-
nection of body organs, food, and their symbolic representations
exemplifies the medieval conception of *fin'amour*, a conception
that privileges the heart as not only the seat of passions and
emotions but also the site of knowledge. Thus, the "sweet taste"
(*douce saveur*) of love is both a matter of taste (*sabor*, to taste)
and a matter of knowledge (*saber*, to know).[1] In this context, it

is not surprising that the Lady of Fayel expresses her surprise and satisfaction when she consumes the heart of her dead lover: "She praised this dish, and it seemed to her that she had never eaten anything more savory, and she said, 'Why and how doesn't our cook prepare it more often? Is it so expensive to prepare such a dish that we can't have it more often? It seems truly delicious to me.'"[2] This feature of the narrative links a number of stories and texts and distinguishes most of the medieval texts from the later, devout versions of the legend of the eaten heart, for the explicit articulation of pleasure of the lady consuming the hidden organ of her lover amounts to a surreptitious enactment of their sexual relation.

Triumph of Love, Triumph of Death

We encounter this feature in a simple yet highly instructive text. It is the ninth story of the Fourth Day of Boccaccio's *Decameron*, written in the fourteenth century.[3] Two knights "who love each other with an exceeding love" live in relative proximity to each other. Guillaume de Guardestaing falls in love with his best friend's lady, the wife of Guillaume de Roussillon. The two lovers go on undiscovered for a while, until, through an indiscretion, de Roussillon learns of their affair and decides to avenge his honor and kill his best friend, now turned dreaded rival. One day, he ambushes de Gaurdestaing and kills him, then tears his heart from his body. He instructs his cook to prepare the heart and to "make a dainty dish thereof, the best and most delectable to eat that you know" (352). He then proceeds to serve the disguised heart to his wife. The husband, however, hides the identity of the heart even from his cook. He tells the cook that the heart belonged to a wild boar, an animal he hunted, and therefore, by designating his dead rival as an animal, a beast subject to hunting, he separates himself from his former friend by redefining the identity of the dead lover.

In contrast to both the *Lai d'Ignaure* and the *Roman du châtelain de Couci,* the meal, in Boccaccio's story, is a private one. Only Guillaume de Roussillon and his wife participate, and the heart, as expected, is fed to the wife alone. He, however, does not eat anything at all; he simply watches and observes his wife consume the heart of her lover. The wife expresses her pleasure and satisfaction with the meal, after which Guillaume proceeds to inform her that he has killed her lover and fed her his heart. She then throws herself from the window and falls to her death, her body broken into pieces.

Before dying, however, she denounces his crime and accuses him of betrayal: "You have done the deed of a disloyal and base knight, which you are; for, if I, unforced by him, made him lord of my love and therein offended against you, not he, but I should have borne the penalty thereof. But God forfend that ever other victual should follow upon such noble meat as the heart of so valiant and so courteous a gentleman as was Sir Guillaume de Gaurdestaing!" (353). Her accusation identifies the violence of her husband's revenge as misplaced and thus names his ignorance and failure to understand the basic structure of reciprocity of love. The elimination of the rival does not produce the desired return to the past. Instead, it puts an end to the marriage and leads to the final reunion of the two dead lovers. Her death, furthermore, while proclaiming the heart as the last meal she will accept, ends with the dispersal and dismemberment of her own body. Her body is made whole only when she is reunited with the dismembered body of her lover in the sepulcher. Guillaume de Roussillon is forced to leave his own land.

Boccaccio's version of this tale highlights the asymptotic relationship between the two male rivals: they are both named

Guillaume, distinguished only by their geographical identifications. Their problematic proximity facilitates their interchangeability and substitution. Geographical distance is reduced here to the absolute minimum while retaining the power to name and identify. And in this case, it is the husband who actually kills his rival and extracts his heart from his body. The two Guillaumes are like twins separated only by land and the desire of the lady. Their shifting relationship mirrors the shifting status and transformations of the heart. Once again, the desire for absolute reciprocity is denied because of a prior discursive contract that excludes one of the participants. Once again the heart undergoes a series of transformations and disguises, culminating in its literalization. The final reunion of the two dead lovers leads to the absolute exclusion and exile of the murderous husband, and thus the closure of the narrative celebrates the triumph of love over the violence of jealousy and envy. The identity of each of the participants is determined by the relative status of the heart and its transmission. The distance between what is offered and what is taken never manages to overcome the gap established by the discursive contract marking the differences between the interested parties. In this perspective, Boccaccio's version condenses the dynamics laid down in the *Roman du châtelain de Couci* by combining that story with some of the features of the *Lai d'Ignaure*. By selecting and rewriting the two previous versions, Boccaccio brings them together in a single, unified narrative.

Another important feature of Boccaccio's text is the absence of any participants during the meal. The private aspect of this perverse dinner is significant because it emphasizes the movement away from the public display of vengeance and the elimination of all witnesses and accomplices. The shift from the public to the private sphere accompanies the reduction of the spatial distance separating the rivals and heralds the reorientation and redefinition of the structure and representational powers of the narratives of the legend of the eaten heart. A second Boccaccian story illustrates and highlights such structural and conceptual shifts. It is the story of Tancred, the story that opens the Fourth Day of the *Decameron,* the day devoted to "those whose loves had an unhappy ending" by Philostrato, whose name means "overcome by love."

Tancred's story violently shatters all the conventions we have encountered so far in the narratives of the legend of the eaten heart. It transfers the conflict between husband and lover to the inner circle of the family and substitutes incest, or, to be more precise, an uncontrollable incestuous desire, for the rivalry between husband and lover. Tancred's only daughter, Ghismonda, after a brief marriage, returns to her father's household after the death of her husband. Her father refuses to give her away in marriage. After some time, she falls secretly in love with Guiscardo, one of her father's servants. Finally, she decides to declare her passion to her secret lover. Unable to confront him in person with her passion and afraid of revealing her love to anyone, "she wrote him a letter, wherein she showed him how he should do to foregather with her on the ensuing day, and placing it in the hollow of a cane, gave the latter jestingly to Guiscardo, saying, 'You will make you a bellows of this for your servingmaid, with which she may blow up the fire tonight'" (294–295). Guiscardo opens the cane, reads the letter, and rejoices. The two lovers finally meet in Ghismonda's room by way of a tunnel and consummate their mutual passion. One day, Tancred enters his daughter's room unannounced and awaits the return of Ghismonda. While waiting he falls asleep on a hassock at the foot of his daughter's bed. Then Ghismonda returns and, not knowing that her father is already in her room, prepares to meet her secret lover: "Without perceiving that there was someone there, [she] opened the secret door to Guiscardo, who was awaiting her. They straightaway betook themselves to bed, as of their wont, and while they sported and solaced themselves together, it befell that Tancred awoke and heard and saw that which Guiscardo and his daughter did: whereat beyond measure grieved, at first he would have cried out at them, but then bethought himself to keep silence and remain, if he might, hidden, so that with more secrecy and less shame to himself he might avail to do that which had already occurred to his mind" (296–297).

Later that night, Tancred orders two of his men to seize Guiscardo and hold him prisoner. He then goes to confront his daughter and ask her to explain her actions. He expresses to her his shock and dismay at her having chosen a lover of the meanest condition, as well as his indecision about what actions he might take to punish her and her secret lover. Ghismonda explains to her father that Guiscardo is her chosen lover and that she did not choose him lightly, despite his lower social standing. Furthermore, she accuses her father of cruelty because he had not allowed her to remarry. Her argument is worth citing here because it signals a significant conceptual shift in the justification of her love:

It should have been manifest to you, Tancred, being as you are of flesh and blood, that you had begotten a daughter of flesh and blood and not of iron or stone; and you should have remembered and should still remember, for all you are old, what and what like are the laws of youth and with what potency they work; nor, albeit you, being a man, have in your best years exercised yourself in part in arms, should you the less know what leisure and luxury can do in the old, to say nothing of the young. I am then, as being of you begotten, of flesh and blood and have lived so little that I am yet young and (for the one and the other reason) full of carnal desire, whereunto the having aforetime, by reason of marriage, known what pleasure it is to give accomplishment to such desire has added marvelous strength. Unable, therefore, to withstand the potency of my desires, I addressed myself, being young and a woman, to follow that which they prompted me and became enamored. (299)

Ghismonda's discourse appeals to the powers of carnal desire and experience. Having been married, she cannot suppress or forget the pleasures of the flesh, and thus she chose a lover for herself. Furthermore, she reminds her father that she is, like him, a creature of flesh and blood, and, like him, she has her own desires. She asserts her independence and autonomy in the name of the laws of nature, and thus her defense of her secret affair is turned into an accusation of her father's cruelty and negligence. Her appeal to "carnal laws" reveals Tancred's secret infatuation with his daughter and shifts the blame and guilt from the lovers to the jealous father. The law of nature and that of youth take precedence over the perverse desires of the old Tancred. The confrontation between father and daughter becomes, in Boccaccio's narrative, an opportunity to argue the case for the supremacy of love and its power to overcome social differences: "But now let us look somewhat to the first principles of things, whereby you will see that we all get our flesh from one same stock and that all souls were by one same Creator created with equal faculties, equal powers and equal virtues. Worth it was that first distinguished between us, who were all and still are born equal; wherefore those who had and used the greatest sum thereof were called noble and the rest abode not noble" (300). Ghismonda's invocation of Christian ideals and principles becomes the vehicle for a critique of the social order itself. Her love literally liberates her from her social and familial condition and returns her to an original and just one.

It is remarkable that this acute although somewhat naive critique of social injustice is made possible by the reduction of the spatial limits and constraints of the conflict to the order of the familial and private. We are no longer confined in the space of the castle, with its order and hierarchy; instead we are in a space delimited and defined by individuals, with their differing motivations and desires. This "individualism" marks a radical departure from the earlier medieval narratives and points to the new and more complex conditions governing the violence brought about by jealousy and rivalry.

Tancred, despite the passionate words of his daughter, cannot overcome his jealousy and his desire to be the sole possessor of Ghismonda. He orders his men to strangle Guiscardo. He then has them extract Guiscardo's heart from his body, places the organ in a golden bowl, and sends it to his daughter, who, in the meantime, has prepared poison in order to end her own life. Upon receipt of the heart, Ghismonda puts it to her lips; she kisses the dead heart an infinite number of times and prepares for her death. And then,

> the lady, having wept as much as seemed fit to her, raised her head and drying her eyes, said, "O, much loved heart, I have accomplished my every office towards you, nor is there left me aught else to do save to come with my soul and bear you company." So saying, she called for the vial wherein was the water she had made the day before and poured the latter into the bowl where was the heart bathed with so many of her tears; then, setting her mouth thereto without any fear, she drank it all off and having drunken, mounted, with the bowl in her hand, upon the bed, where composing her body as most decently as she might, she pressed her lover's heart to her own and without saying aught, awaited death. (303)

Ghismonda's final act constitutes her ultimate revenge. Her devotion to her dead lover negates and rejects her father's desires. She chooses to die on her own bed, the scene of her love as well as the locus of her father's jealousy and the object of his incestuous desire. Her last symbolic reunion with her dead lover seeks to abolish the distance separating the dead and the living, the dismembered body and the body awaiting and desiring the mutilated organ. Ghismonda's death scene is also a mourning scene. Before she drinks the poison mixed with her tears and the liquid of her lover's heart, she makes sure that she mourns Guiscardo in public, in front of her ladies. Her desire to announce and show her mourning is not only a confirmation of her love in the face of her father's wishes and demands, it is also a necessary step in order for her to assert the fundamental equality between her and her dead lover. The heart, in this instance, is no longer an object to be eaten. It is not and cannot be disguised. Instead of a last meal, the death scene follows and obeys carnal laws, the laws of desire and the flesh. The heart is not eaten because the love affair is just. The heart is not eaten because the relationship between Ghismonda and Guiscardo does not transgress any human laws, and it is opposed to the unnatural and perverse incestuous desires of the father. The conflict motivating the rivalry between the husband and the lover that we encountered in the *Roman du châtelain de Couci* and the *Lai d'Ignaure* is here transformed and replaced by the conflict between father and daughter. The lover is merely the outside agent, the necessary third party that brings to life and forces a resolution of the opposition between father and daughter. Guiscardo's heart is served to Ghismonda raw, in its natural state and condition, as if to highlight the powers and vicissitudes of the flesh. The naked heart becomes the object of devotion, but it also calls for the other body with all its desires. Thus, Ghismonda's tears literally, according to the text, cover up and engulf the heart of the dead lover. Undisguised and raw, the heart can only accept the clear liquid that mourns its loss but also affirms and celebrates its carnal pleasures. Tears, in effect, become the active substitute for desire at the conclusion of the tale. The tears shed by Ghismonda over her lover's heart blind her eyes and reenact her last reunion with Guiscardo before Tancred's voyeuristic intrusion. Vision and the eyes, the agents of jealousy and violence, become Ghismonda's only resort and her last weapon against her father's cruelty.

Ghismonda's last words to her father confirm her rejection of his desires by rejecting his tears: "Tancred, keep these tears against a less desired fate than this of mine and give them not to me, who desire them not. Who ever saw any, other than you, lament for that which he himself has willed? Nevertheless, if aught yet live in you of the love which once you bore me, vouchsafe me for a last boon that, since it was not your pleasure that I should privily and in secret live with Guiscardo, my body may openly abide with his, wheresoever you have caused him to be cast dead" (303). Her last words are a double request: first, for her father to overcome his incestuous desire and to return to his "original" and natural love for her as a daughter; second, for him to allow the heart of her dead lover, now intertwined with hers on her deathbed, to rejoin its body, and thus for her to rest with the body of her dead Guiscardo.

Dante's Eaten Heart

Boccaccio's two tales introduce a number of important changes into the structure of the narratives of the legend of the eaten heart. They describe the shift from the enclosed spaces of the early medieval castle to the private spaces inhabited by autonomous individuals with conflicting wills and desires. They also displace the surreptitious substitution of food and the heart by introducing new representations that exploit different social categories. The retreat to the private, however, was not an innovation of the author of the *Decameron*. This retreat finds its first and most important expression in a text by Dante, a text whose form celebrates and interrogates the private: his autobiography. I will turn now to what is perhaps the most unusual text in the tradition of the legend of the eaten heart, a text that takes us back to the Dionysian heritage of the legend and its neoplatonic and Christian ramifications.

The third chapter of Dante's *Vita Nuova* (written in the late thirteenth century) contains the description of a remarkable vision. One afternoon, Dante encounters Beatrice on a certain street:

> She turned her eyes to where I was standing faint-hearted and, with that indescribable graciousness for which today she is rewarded in the eternal life, she greeted me so miraculously that I seemed at that moment to behold the entire range of possible bliss. It was precisely the ninth hour of that day, three o'clock in the afternoon, when her sweet greeting came to me. Since this was the first time her words had ever been directed to me, I became so ecstatic that, like a drunken man, I turned away from everyone and I sought the loneliness of my room, where I began thinking of this most gracious lady and, thinking of her, I fell into a sweet sleep, and a marvelous vision appeared to me. I seemed to see a cloud the color of fire and, in that cloud, a lordly man, frightening to behold, yet he seemed also to be wondrously filled with joy. He spoke and said many things, of which I understood only a few; one was *Ego dominus tuus* [I am thy master]. I seemed to see in his arms a sleeping figure, naked but lightly wrapped in a crimson cloth; looking intently at this figure, I recognized the lady of the greeting, the lady who earlier in the day had deigned to greet me. In one hand he seemed to be holding something that was all in flames, and it seemed to me that he said these words: *Vide cor tuum* [Behold your heart]. And after some time had passed, he seemed to awaken the one who slept, and he forced her cunningly to eat of that burning object in his hand; she ate of it timidly. A short time after this, his happiness gave way to bitterest weeping, and weeping he folded his arms around this lady, and together they seemed to ascend toward the heavens. (5–6)[4]

This phantasmagoric consumption of the burning heart marks a crucial moment in Dante's narrative in the *Vita Nuova* and in the development of his poetics. Dante's vision contains a number of inversions and reversals that frame the content of the "vision" and link it to the situation that seems to have produced it. Dante's sleep, initiated by the power of Beatrice's words, gives the image of a mute and sleeping Beatrice, a passive Beatrice who is forced to eat part of the poet's burning heart. He is identified in the vision by his heart and by the naming of the burning heart as his. The act of eating the heart is also initiated from the outside by the lord who holds it in his hand. This time, however, the heart is no longer disguised; instead, it is itself being consumed by the flames and Beatrice simply eats parts of it. More important, Dante's position seems to mirror that of the lover, and the lord holding his heart remotely echoes the husband's position. The partial consumption of the heart sets Dante's vision apart from the rest. It suggests an incompleteness and the lack of closure, a lack that, in a sense, will generate Dante's poetic structure, culminating in the reunion in the heavens with the absent and lost body of Beatrice. It will also culminate in his recovery of his own identity.

Dante, in his vision, is a witness to the revelation of his destiny and true identity. He is simply an observer, a passive participant like the sleeping Beatrice. As such, his vision remotely recalls the mirror of Dionysus and his loss in his quest for the reflection of his true image and identity. But it also is a narcissistic variation on the Dionysian mirror. Dante's vision, in part because of its trinitarian structure, eliminates the diversity and multiplicity generated by the Dionysian sacrifice and opts instead for a redefined narcissistic reflection. Between the two mirrors, between Dionysus and his fate and Narcissus and his tragic nostalgia, Dante's vision grafts and traces its own development and unfolding. It is as if Dante's vision interiorizes the Dionysian mirror under the guise and disguise of the narcissistic in order to ground the emergence of the poetic project it inaugurates. Between the two spaces, the public and the private, the collective and the individual, lie the innovation and the originality of Dante's vision. Dante's unique position, both as witness and as a passive participant in a scene of desire and transcendence, displaces and re-

defines the figurative status of the heart and its consumption by
Beatrice.

And it is no coincidence that all this is framed and generated
by a simple salutation, words of greeting but also of recognition
and identification. Dante's vision appears to mirror another salutation, that of the Annunciation, in the manner in which it sets
forth the miraculous birth of its poetic manifestation and the
celebration of the lady as the most privileged agency for such a
generation. Whereas in the Annunciation it is the angel Gabriel
who salutes Mary, here, in Dante's autobiography, it is Beatrice
who salutes the poet. This reversal is crucial, for it signals the
incorporation and the displacement of the narrative elements of
the Annunciation into the story leading to the poet's vision and
its ensuing narrative of the quest for interpretation. Dante's
poetic trajectory is fully inscribed within this initial and all-deter-
mining encounter with the power of Beatrice's words. The trinitarian structure of the vision, itself reinforced and repeated three
times within the *Vita Nuova,* leaves Dante wanting to rejoin his
lady and part of himself. In order to do so he has to undertake
the quest which is the journey of the *Divine Comedy.* Dante's
vision, inaugurated by simple words of salutation, announces a
beginning that already inscribes its closure within its own space
and therefore makes it necessary for the poet to undergo a series
of experiences leading to its epiphanic fulfillment.

Dante's vision constitutes a radical departure from the conventional articulations of the legend of the eaten heart and its
inscription within a framework defined by the Eucharist and the
cult of the Sacred Heart and locates its generative powers in an
environment that heralds the emergence of a specific poetic
identity and subjectivity. For the immediate impact of the vision
consists in the writing of a sonnet that describes the vision and
asks for an interpretation of its meaning and content. The vision
thus gives rise to lyrical production, and the sonnet detaches the

vision from its immediate context and circulates it in a community of poets, a community founded on a common interest in love and its poetic economy: "Musing on what I had seen, I decided to make it known to many of the famous poets of the times. Since recently I had discovered my abilities as a poet, I resolved to compose a sonnet in which I would address all Love's faithful subjects; and requesting them to interpret my vision, I wrote to them everything that I had seen in my sleep" (III:6). Dante's vision, grounded in a structure of revelation and annunciation, makes it possible for him to insert himself into the community of poets, the community defined and ruled by the Lord of Love, and thus operates the transfer from the private to the public, from the personal to the communal. The sonnet itself inscribes the poetic exercise as a form of revelation but also as the articulation of the desire to join the new community. Dante's opening sonnet of his autobiography inaugurates his poetic journey and presents this inauguration in the form of a question and a request. Furthermore, the structure of the sonnet itself reinscribes the vision and actualizes its impact on the poet. In other words, the lyrical reformulation of the vision becomes the fertile ground for the expression of the poet's identity. Here is the sonnet:

> To every captive soul and loving heart
> To whom these words I have composed are sent
> For your elucidation in reply,
> Greetings I bring for your sweet lord's sake, Love.
> The first three hours, the hours of the time
> Of shining stars, were coming to an end,
> When suddenly Love appeared before me
> (To remember how he really was appalls me).
> Joyous, Love seemed to me, holding my heart
> Within his hand, and in his arms he had
> My lady, loosely wrapped in folds, asleep.
> He woke her then, and gently fed to her

The burning heart; she ate it, terrified.
And then I saw them disappear in tears.
(III:6)

The vision, originally occasioned by simple words of greeting
from Beatrice, in its lyrical form becomes words of greeting
addressed to the community of poets. Beatrice's words of greeting led to the poet's sleep, and his sonnet produces a quest for
meaning and interpretation. The text shifts from narrative to lyric,
from the passive state of the sleeper to the active desire for
recognition and interpretation on the part of the poet. The *Ego
dominus tuus* of the vision has now been interpreted by Dante as
his poetic vocation. The transformation of the vision into the
founding moment of the *Vita Nuova*, thanks to its lyrical interpretation and reformulation, finds its closure in new forms and
modes of communication and discursive exchange: "This sonnet
was answered by many possessing a variety of opinions, among
them was the one I call my first friend, who composed a sonnet
which begins: 'I think that you beheld all worth.' My sending
the sonnet to him resulted in the forming of our friendship"
(III:7). The poet's eaten heart, as a result of its trajectory from
the visionary to the lyrical, opens the door for the ideal form of
subjective communication: friendship. The poetic reaction to the
terrifying vision is thus domesticated and neutralized through
dialogic discursive exchange and interpretation. The secret of the
vision, initially inaccessible, reveals itself and opens up its mystery
thanks to the lyrical temporality and interpretation of poetry:
"The true interpretation of the dream I described was not perceived by anyone then, but now it is very clear even to the least
sophisticated" (III:7). Dante's eaten heart translates into his
lyrical words, into words that describe their subject as an object
of carnal and cannibalistic consumption while offering themselves
to the temporality and work of interpretation. The Lord of Love,

initially controlling and possessing Dante's body in the vision, has now become the medium and intermediary for his poetic self-description, the impetus for his autobiographical narrative and the discovery and pursuit of his poetic vocation. The emergence of friendship as a result of the quest for meaning and interpretation concludes the closure of the poetic and lyrical appropriation and the transfiguration of the inner and private revelation of the poet's subjectivity and identity. Friendship, the ideal of communication and discursive exchange, now comes to replace the private revelation of the vision. The move from the private, imaginary world to the realm of discursive friendship is accompanied by the domestication of Beatrice, that is, by her exclusion as a powerful presence and her reduction to an object of discursive exchange and representation. She has now become the locus of Dante's poetry, the end of his lyrical quest; and along the way on his journey, Dante will reveal himself to his friend and thus to himself. Friendship comes to take the place of the uncontrollable powers of the dream, and the Lord of Love, initially possessing the heart of the poet, has now been transformed into his poetic master, his guide into the world of poetry and friendship.

Mirrors of Friendship

The grounding of such a subjectivity completely moves away from the interpersonal space established by parody and rivalry, the same mirroring rivalry we encountered in the early versions of the legend of the eaten heart. This move inaugurated by Dante toward the institution of a new subjectivity, a new type of interpersonal space, is succinctly articulated by Bacon in his essay "On Friendship": "The parable of Pythagoras is dark, but true: *Cor ne edito,* 'Eat not the heart.' Certainly, if a man would give it a hard phrase, those that want friends to open themselves unto are cannibals of their own hearts. But one thing that is most admirable (wherewith I will conclude the first fruit of friendship), which is, that communicating of a man's self to his friends works two contrary effects, for it redoubleth joys, and cutteth griefs in half."[5] Bacon's calculus of the self, occasioned by and grounded in the Pythagorean dictum, seeks to avoid a most dangerous case, a "disease of stoppings and suffocation," the all-terrifying and destructive anthropophagy. The dreaded anthropophagy here names the heart as the locus of communication and the organ, in and through discursive exchange, that lies at the foundation of a community, of a select collectivity defined by its discursive negotiation with active communication. Bacon's invocation of the dark Pythagorean parable, in a manner reminiscent of Dante's vision, strips the narrative behind the parable of its theological and cultic framework, extracting it from its dietary and theological context in order to reconfigure it in terms of the interrelations between self and other, between self and discourse. The shared experience of friendship substitutes discourse for the act of eating and identifies language as the means of recognizing and perhaps overcoming alterity.

The absence of friends necessitates a dangerous turn within, a turn that eliminates the possibility of any discursive communication and therefore contaminates the body and devours the self. Speaking to a friend is the equivalent of breathing. It is the sustenance of life. And this is so because it makes it possible to exteriorize the heart, the seat of the self within the body. Such exteriorization, within the private space of friendship, literally opens the heart, that is, it makes visible what is only a figure of the self. In other words, we have traveled from the original Pythagorean *Cor ne edito* to the transfiguration of the biblical *Vide cor tuum* in Dante's vision and its generation of the lyrical quest for interpretation and friendship. We have come full circle, from the initial prohibition to the most exhibitionist desire, from the removal of the heart as an edible object to its offering under the guise and disguise of linguistic communication, from the prohibition dictating what can and cannot be shared as food to the will to share all and everything, and above all one's self.

Bacon's friendship, in its Pythagorean definition, transforms the body of the interlocutor into a privileged space for the exchange and circulation of words. The body emerges as a place for writing and speaking, a scene of discursive definitions and manipulations whose principal aim is to avoid the absence of words with their healing powers. The new dynamics of the body, grounded in friendship, operates and informs the institution of discourse as the vital principle for the survival of the body. Silence, in this context, is the most dangerous condition of all, for it inflects the absence of any possibility of exteriorization into the decay of the desiring words into powerful instruments that threaten to wound and devour the body. Silence, or the absence of an appropriate and qualified interlocutor—a true friend—splits the self into competing parts and reduces the body to a scene of violence and cannibalistic drives. The discourse made possible by friendship, the discourse that is friendship itself, allows for a sharing of experiences thanks to and through words and thus invents a new space in which the dangerous and threatening words move and circulate. The ultimate desire for friendship is a desire for survival, for the survival of the body as the source of obscure and secret powerful words. Therefore friendship, in Bacon's essay, takes on a magical status. It becomes, in effect, the equivalent of the philosopher's stone: "For there is no man that imparteth his joys to his friend, but he joyeth the more; and no man that imparteth his griefs to his friend, but he grieveth the less. So that it is in truth of operation upon a man's mind, of like virtue as the alchemists use to attribute to their stone for man's body, that it worketh all contrary effects, but still to the good and benefit of nature" (141).

Friendship, the philosopher's stone of words, neutralizes the dangers inherent in words when they are not shared with a true friend. Language and discourse, the act of communication itself, double and duplicate the self. The multiplication of the self, the creation of a mirror image of one's own self, constitutes the radical achievement of friendship because it allows for the expansion of the body and its desires through the interpersonal space of communication. It is ultimately this mirroring that explains Bacon's resort to the Pythagorean dictum. The cannibalistic act underlying Pythagoras' words implies a violent desire to kill and eliminate the young god Dionysus, to literally erase all traces of his body, whereas friendship seeks to duplicate the self, to reproduce an image of the self and to reflect an image of the other that is itself the same. In this perspective, anthropophagy amounts either to extreme narcissism, the self devouring the self for the lack of any recognizable other, or to immersion and loss into a sea of other selves. The heart is thus a mirror. It is indeed the mirror par excellence, for it now reflects the most hidden desires and the most powerful drives of the inner self. The heart is a container, a receptacle where things take shape and form and await their discursive articulation, their transformation and liberation by and through words. The heart marks the emergence of the self from its narcissistic abyss into the world of communication. The heart remains the principle and the site of life; it remains the locus of the vital being of the self, but it is now open to the other, to exteriority and its liberating powers through the discourse that is friendship. Thus, "a man hath a body, and that body is confined to a place; but where friendship is, all offices of life are as it were granted to him and his deputy, for he may exercise them by his friend" (144). Friendship extends the body; it doubles it because it opens up the heart and displays its most inner contents to the true other-self.

Pythagoras' *Cor ne edito* prohibited the eating of human flesh in the name of a community, in the name of the universal principle of life that unifies all its forms and resides in the human heart. The Christian *Hoc est corpus meum* offered the mystical body of Christ as the ultimate act of eating that has the power to neutralize and reverse that other disastrous moment of eating at the origin of human history. In the Eucharist, the communal dimension of the offering transcends individuality in order to achieve the salvation of the human race. Dante's *Vide cor tuum* and Bacon's transformation of the Pythagoreans' *Cor ne edito* celebrate a different and emergent form of community, a community founded on the individual's drives and desires, on the poet's quest for closure, and on the ultimate determining role performed by linguistic manipulation and discursive production. The new community heralded by Dante and celebrated by Bacon is a community first and foremost of individuals, of individual speaking subjects. Bacon's ideal community itself is constituted as a body, a corpus with its organs subject to illness and healing: "We know diseases of stoppings and suffocations are the most dangerous in the body; and it is not much otherwise in the mind: you may take sarza to open the liver, steel to open the spleen, flowers of sulphur for the lungs, castoreum for the brain; but no receipt openeth the heart but a true friend" (144). The heart is now the key to the mind and the soul, and the key to the heart is its opening, that is, its exteriorization and visualization in a discursive exchange and offering. The opening of the heart, its being made public in this most private affair that is friendship, requires the presence of an other, an interlocutor who is capable of understanding and bringing out the thoughts and words that haunt and inhabit the heart. The structure of friendship, grounded as it is in the desire and necessity to overcome the mortal threats of silence that transform words into wounds of the heart, institutes a modality of exchange, an economy of transfer and substitution between the two members constitutive of friendship. In Bacon's text, this substitution and transfer are occasioned to a large degree by the dread of cannibalism. Friendship, in its effective intervention into the domain of the heart, serves as a protection against anthropophagy, and the calculus of the self that ensues is only there in order to account for and explain the ways in which friendship, as discourse, avoids the pitfalls of anthropophagy.

The calculus of the self constitutive of friendship is not unique to Bacon's text; it is a commonplace in the discourse on friendship. The originality of Bacon's essay lies in the articulation of this calculus in terms of the heart and its cannibalistic economy. Bacon thus succeeds in introducing a new dimension into the traditions and conventions of the discourse on friendship, a dimension that sets his essay apart from the other classical texts dealing with the same issue. Montaigne in his essay on friendship, by recalling and marshaling the classical discourse on friendship, deploys a version of the calculus of the self. Montaigne's text aims first and foremost at distinguishing friendship from all other human relations: parenthood, marriage, and so forth. Friendship is unique precisely because, in a certain sense, it does not involve any other self. Or to be more precise, it is unique because it involves an other self that is ultimately not other. This is what Montaigne refers to as the miracle of friendship: "For this perfect friendship of which I speak is indivisible; each gives himself so entirely to his friend, that nothing is left him to spread elsewhere; on the other hand, he is unsatisfied that he not be double, triple or quadruple, and that he not have several souls and several wills that he may devote them all to this subject . . . A unique and principal friendship undoes all other obligations. The secret that I have sworn not to reveal to any other I can, without committing perjury, communicate to the one who is not other than I: he is I."[6] The miracle of friendship, the doubling of the self without any change whatsoever, allows Montaigne to establish friendship as the unique and most privileged form of human relation. It also accounts for the figurative structure of the essay on friendship in Montaigne's book of essays and the radical difference between his text and Bacon's. For, in the case of Montaigne, friendship is also primarily a specific, historically real friendship, namely his relation to La Boétie, and the rest of the discourse on friendship derives from this absolute condition. Bacon's essay, on the other hand, is conceived and written as an essay on friendship in general, on its possibility and potential, its modalities and variations, without any immediate references implicating the author or narrator of the text. Furthermore, Bacon's essay transcends the commonplace references to antiquity and classical texts by introducing the Pythagorean fable at the center of his argumentation. The impact of the emergence of a discourse on cannibalism in the general context of friendship sets Bacon's essay apart. It also echoes a number of religious and theological texts that discuss anthropophagy—echoes, but only as a distant whisper. I will limit myself here to one example.

An Economy of Resurrection

Augustine, in *De Civitate Dei,* provides an interesting discussion of cannibalism in terms that are close to parts of Bacon's text. In trying to answer the difficult question of the resurrection of a man whose body or parts of his body were eaten by another during a famine, Augustine reverts to monetary metaphors that inscribe cannibalism in terms of an intriguing form of exchange and circulation of the body and its parts: "Any flesh that starvation stripped off from the hungry man evidently exhaled into the air, and the Creator, as I said, has the power to bring it back from the air. And so the other flesh will be restored to the man in whom it first began to be human flesh. We must reckon the other man to have borrowed it; and like borrowed money, it has to be given back to the place from which it was taken [*Ab illo quippe altero tamquam mutuo sumpta deputanda est; quae sicut aes alienum ei redhibenda est, unde sumpta est*]. And this man's flesh, which starvation has stripped from him, will be restored to him by the one who can bring back even what has been exhaled into the air."[7]

Augustine's answer to "this most difficult question" is not at all surprising. It continues, in fact, a long-established tradition of Christian interpretation of resurrection and its modalities. What is striking and unique are precisely the terms of the answer, that is, the monetary metaphor and its theological implications. For Augustine, God occupies the position of an absolute banker who controls and oversees the growth and exchange of human flesh from its creation to death and resurrection.[8] Furthermore, Augustine avoids addressing directly the issue of anthropophagy, for he appears to insist that starvation is the guilty party and is thus the actual consumer of the flesh of the other.

The circularity of the system of the circulation of flesh, despite its transitory transformation, its perfect closure without any loss or remainder whatsoever, constitutes the necessary element for the successful divine intervention. Flesh—the currency and agency of creation and of God the creator and his creatures, the element of exchange between the creator, nature, and his creation—admits of no absolute transformation or transfiguration. It has no room for permanent change. Instead, it intensifies and illustrates the absolute mastery of the creator over his creatures in all its possible manifestations. The economy of anthropophagy, in Augustine's text, calls for a strict and restricted economy of the flesh, of the matter of the earth and humanity so that God can ascertain and affirm his powers. But in order for him to do so, he has to recover, at least in theoretical terms, any flesh that has become the subject of perverse loss or consumption.

The pressing literality of the exchange, its striking but perfectly comprehensible insistence on absolute closure, marks the physical body as the playground and theater for God's domination and manipulation of the flesh of his creatures. It is also the place where God the creator has to demonstrate his absolute power, his ability to bring back what has been detached, consumed, and transformed by cannibalism. The calculus of the divine recuperation of the flesh that constitutes resurrection demarcates the body, in its most material manifestation, as the locus of the fall and of loss. It inscribes flesh as the vehicle for transfer and transformation. In the same manner that God will manifest himself in the flesh, so also human flesh will regain its origin in the originary and continuous act of incorporation masterminded by the Creator. The economy of resurrection is grounded in the Augustinian eschatology and the special place the physical body occupies in this eschatology. It is also grounded, for the intelligibility and centrality of the economc model, in the founding contractual relation between man and his creator, between the believer and his god. The founding act of faith, the originary contract tying the community of believers in their special relations to the Creator, is none other than a *symbolum,* that is, a verbal and linguistic contract modeled on the ancient practice of commerce and forms of exchange. The structure underlying the articulation and expression of faith itself reproduces the model of exchange and reunification, based on commercial and monetary elements, that forms the unity and union of the community of believers. *Symbolum,* the recitation of the articles of Christian faith and, as Augustine would say, the inscription of these articles in the hearts of the believers, mirrors and echoes the economy of recovery of the lost and misplaced flesh. In theological terms, it grounds the model according to which cannibalism is negated through the powers of divine intervention into the realm of human flesh. Christianity, in symbolic terms, thus puts an end to cannibalism and anthropophagy by introducing a new allegorical

Saint Augustine holding his flaming heart.

form of exchange, a new figurative structure of debt and payment—in short, a new economy of the self and its flesh and their relation to the Creator. Augustine's discussion of cannibalism, in this context, merely supplies the proof and sets the norm for the Christian argumentation and demonstration of the powers of the divine and its absolute domination of the affairs of the flesh.

The discourse on friendship in Bacon's text, grounded as it is in the centrality of the figurative status of the human heart and the forms of transfer and exchange it makes possible, seems to absorb and swallow the divine calculus of resurrection under the form of a calculus of the self and its desires to mirror itself in the other.

God, the ultimate and absolute financial speculator, allows no speculation whatsoever. His currency, his money, the tool of his trade, so to speak, is flesh, human flesh, the substance that emanates from him but is no longer exactly like him. The circulation of flesh, its interiorization as food and its consequent exhalation into the air, require a divine intervention, a restorative operation that will return the lost and wandering flesh to the original body from which it was detached. The economy of cannibalism in Augustine's text is fundamentally a nostalgic drive and desire, a nostalgia for the origin and the plenitude of the original state of creation. The emergence of monetary and economic metaphors, along with their juridical and legal context, testifies to the desire for restitution, that is, a return to a prior state. Augustine's text, therefore, implicates cannibalism and its resolution as another manifestation of the powers of the divine.

Bacon's essay becomes, in this perspective, a remarkable document that translates this divine economy, motivated by a nostalgic desire for a necessary and inevitable reunion with the origin, into a human economy, grounded in discourse and the healing powers of words. The flesh that circulated through space and time awaiting the reunion with the body on the last day now has become the words, residing in the heart and awaiting an occasion and an interlocutor in order to be uttered and exhaled into the rarefied air of friendship. The heart is not only the locus of friendship and communication; it is also a fully active microcosm that replaces the universe in which flesh traveled. The heart, the vehicle of the self in and through discourse, cannot and should not be closed off or sealed off. On the contrary, it needs to be opened up, shown, manifested, expressed, and circulated, among friends to be sure, and only among friends. The shift from a Christian cosmology to a human domain is thus accompanied by an inversion of the modalities of exchange and transfer, an inversion of the ways and manners of recuperation and recovery, of illness and convalescence. The heart, now the center of human relations and the carrier of the true self, is in need of a public, a highly restricted and limited public of one, but a public nevertheless. If Augustine's God can bring back what has been exhaled into the air, Bacon's friend can heal the wounded and sick heart with simple but powerful words.

Cor ne edito: Pythagoras' absolute prohibition is now simply a parable of and for the heart, that is, a linguistic and discursive object in quest of interpretation whose truth lies at the center of new, emerging representations of the body and its organs, of the heart and its figures, of self and identity. Pythagoras' prohibition now names a parabolic form of cannibalism, a figurative transmutation of the body of the other into one's self and of one's self into another body under the guise of friendship. "Eat not the heart," for the heart is what can no longer be eaten because it is inhabited by words that mirror the self in its quest for a friend. In other words, Bacon's heart, in the manner of Dante's Lord of Love, exhibits itself, shows its most inner parts, to the one who mirrors himself in the same fashion by opening up his own heart. The heart, the organ of life and speech, the organ of rebirth and regeneration, the organ of the sacred and the magical, has finally been fully humanized. It has been given to man as the tool and instrument of friendship, as the means of mastering the self and the flesh in and through the words that inhabit the heart.

THREE

A Lover's Course:
"Le Coeur Mangé"

"For everything going in at the mouth, is cast out into the
draught" . . . But with the opening of their eyes referred to,
they made entrance upon the path of death.

IRENAEUS, *AGAINST HERESIES*

Jean-Pierre Camus (1584–1652), bishop of Belley and close
friend and admirer of Saint François de Sales, was one of the most
prolific Christian writers of the first half of the seventeenth century in France.[1] He is the author of more than forty books and
a large collection of short stories, the majority of which depict
unique and somewhat bizarre events. His general objective was
to write an encyclopedic collection of tales that covered the entire
spectrum of human emotions. Behind this monumental undertaking lay Camus's belief in the pedagogical value of narrative
and his conviction that the most appropriate medium for teaching
Christian morality to the general public was the use of short,
exemplary stories from which morals could easily be drawn.[2] Thus
his corpus, in the words of one of his rare modern editors, was
organized in three general parts: "[Camus] organizes this vast

material by distinguishing three kinds of collections: the tragic stories *(les histoires tragiques),* the pleasant and entertaining ones *(les histoires agréables et récréatives),* the unique and exemplary ones which are the most numerous."[3] From this vast and rich material produced by Camus, I will limit myself to the analysis of a tale that tells the story of a perverse case of anthropophagy. "Le Coeur mangé" appeared in the collection of short narratives published by Camus in 1630 under the juicy title, *Les Spectacles d'Horreur où se découvrent plusieurs effets de nostre siècle* ("Spectacles of Horror where can be found several aspects of our century").[4]

In his preface to the volume, Camus informs his readers that the majority of the tales they are about to read are new and original. Even the ones borrowed from the ancient authors, Camus goes on to claim, have been substantially improved: "You will find, reader, in these Spectacles, among the brand-new Stories, some that were already written, and that I assembled in uncommon books that you would have difficulty finding elsewhere. And I can in some manner call them new since if the matter isn't new the manner of telling it is; this is the principal interest of the compositions" (Preface). Camus's claim for the originality of some of his stories directs the reader's attention to their stylistic and literary qualities.[5] He also takes credit for making available a number of stories that are otherwise difficult to find. "Le Coeur mangé," as we shall see, is an ideal case to test the claims put forward by Camus in the preface.[6] Although he presents his story as the narration of recent and actual events, it is most likely that it is simply the result of a reworking and combination of a number of older stories.[7] In fact, this double fictional status of the story constitutes one of the most interesting and revealing aspects of the text in the manner in which it allows Camus to exploit a number of legends and texts dealing with anthropophagy. The "composition," as Camus calls it, consists of a motivated and powerful assimilation of older texts, an assimilation that relies on the resolution of the tension between a Christian morality and a poetics of courtly love.

Woman's Womb and Lover's Sepulcher

On a first reading, Camus's tale of the eaten heart appears to be a very straightforward exposition of the horrors of jealousy and the misguided application of parental authority. Memnon, a young man of modest means, falls in love with Crisele, a beautiful young lady. After much effort and devotion on the part of the young couple, Crisele's parents reluctantly accept the relationship between their daughter and Memnon and promise to marry her to the young man. One day an old and rich gentleman, recently widowed, sees Crisele and falls in love with her beauty. Despite his old age and his previous marriage, Rogat, through the influence of his considerable fortune, persuades Crisele's parents to promise him their daughter for a second wife. Crisele sadly marries Rogat out of respect for her parents' will and authority, and she asks Memnon, whom she still loves, to move to a different part of the country. Memnon, obeying his lover's wishes, enlists in the army and goes to fight in Flanders. After about a year of courageous fighting, Memnon is fatally wounded in battle. Before his death, however, he writes a letter to Crisele and entrusts one of his relatives to take his heart to his lover. Crisele buries the heart in a church and devotes herself to mourning the loss of her lover. Rogat's jealousy is stirred up by his wife's public devotion to her dead lover. One day, he arranges to steal the heart from its grave in the church and instructs his cook to prepare it as a pâté. He then proceeds to feed his wife the heart of her lover. Once Crisele discovers what has happened to Memnon's heart, she informs the relative who had brought it to her, who challenges Rogat and kills him in a duel. Crisele spends the rest of her life in a convent.

The theme of anthropophagy deployed in Camus's text belongs, as we have already seen, to a rich and fascinating medieval tradition that receives its most significant, or at least best known, manifestation in the *Decameron*. Camus's story, however, in its opening gesture ignores its most immediate models and invokes the story of Thyestes, a mythological paradigm that has come to represent and symbolize the horrors associated with anthropophagy. By doing so, the tale seeks to overcome the limits of immediate reference in order to situate itself under the sign of a new frame of reference, the most general of all. Here is the opening paragraph of the text: "You are going to see in this horrible Spectacle, not quite the banquet of Thyestes, but something similar. And you will learn just how far can go the fury of enraged jealousy warring not only with the living, but even with the dead" (28). The legend of Thyestes tells the story of Atreus, who feeds his brother's children to their father. The legend was used by Aeschylus to explain in part the murder of Agamemnon, and Seneca devoted an entire tragedy to the story. Moreover, in sixteenth-century France, the story of Thyestes was often used to describe the schism in the church and the religious wars between the Catholics and the Huguenots. Agrippa d'Aubigné, himself a Huguenot warrior, provides us with the most important instance of this use of the legend of Thyestes in the first section of his poem, *Les Tragiques*:

> The mother having long battled in her heart
> The fire of pity, the furor of hunger,
> Covets in her breast the beloved creature
> And says to her child (less mother than famished):
> "Wretched one, give back, give back the body I made for you;
> Your blood will return to where you took milk,

To the breast that fed you return unnaturally;
This breast that nourished you will be your sepulcher."
Her hand trembles pulling the knife,
When to sacrifice the lamb of her womb,
With her thumb she extends its neck like a chick who coos
A few soft words, thinking it's being caressed:
At the fearful blow, her heart stops.
Twice the steel falls from the hand that stiffens.
All is trouble and confusion in the soul that
Is no more a mother, but all wolf.
From her tarnished lip ardent fires dart,
And kisses changed into avid bites,
She opens the passage to blood and spirits.
The child's face changes and its laughter turns to cries;
It lets out three sighs and, having no more mother,
Dying, seeks with its eyes the eyes of its murderess.
It is said that Thyestes' same act of eating
Blackened and blotted out the sun.
Shall we go further? Do we want to see the rest
Of this banquet of horror, worse than Thyestes'?[8]

Aubigné's moving description of the mother sacrificing her son, of the church murdering some of her children, deplores the violence and horror of civil and religious wars as the effects of a perverse and generalized economy of cannibalism. In this perspective, the story of Thyestes serves as the paradigmatic representation of cannibalism conceived in military terms. Eating human flesh and killing are associated with each other, converging on an allegorical body divided by its internal needs and its conflicting obligations to itself and to the infants it is supposed to nourish and protect. For Aubigné, hunger, the deprivation of the allegorical mother, and the ensuing destruction of the mother's love for her child constitute the tragic elements of his figurative description of religious wars. His reference to Thyestes belongs to a long-established tradition that goes back at least to

Seneca's tragedy with its detailed descriptions of the horrors of anthropophagy. Camus's invocation of Thyestes in the opening sentence of his tale is not necessarily a direct reference to Aubigné's text. But considering that the two authors belonged to two different groups divided by political, and, most important for us, theological conceptions, Camus's text may be viewed as an implicit response to Aubigné's allegorization of the legend of Thyestes.

The reference to the legend of Thyestes in Camus's tale, however, is directly related to military rhetoric, to the representation of a war between the living and the dead, or, more accurately, a war waged by the living on the dead and their potential survival in representation. This military rhetoric appears at first to be merely an instance of the conventional representation of love and jealousy. Memnon, the young hero, "makes a glorious conquest of Crisele's affections" (28–29). This use of a conventional representation of love will surface again at the end of the narrative in a significant manner; for now it suffices to say that the appearance of the military topos in the text is important because it emphasizes the tension and conflict between the various conventions and traditions that Camus is reworking and dislocating in his narrative. In the courtly tradition, for instance, the military representation of passion and love marks the idealization of the woman, an idealization that is always accompanied by an emphasis on the heart as the seat of life and passions as opposed to the body and sexuality. The courtly heart requires an honest and chaste love. This tradition thus highlights the value and valorization of the feminine figure by privileging its inaccessibility and fundamental difference. Memnon's love for Crisele follows this model: his love is spiritual, devoted to her idealized image represented by her heart. It is as if Memnon can only love the Crisele represented by her heart, by the metaphorical powers invested in the heart, since his bond to her is grounded in reciprocity, a reciprocity that forbids any sexual or physical rapport.

Memnon's conquest of Crisele's heart has to be taken literally, for the war between the living and the dead at the center of this narrative focuses on the dual representational models originating in and fighting for the control of the young woman's heart. Thus Rogat's passion for Crisele is described in the following terms: "Rogat, one of the richest and most authoritative gentlemen of the area, having seen in a gathering the beauty of Crisele, capable of dazzling better eyes than his, became so besotted that without thinking that he had enough children from his first marriage and that his advanced age made Venus irreconcilably stand against him, thought that he could not continue to live unless he possessed this beauty which ravished him" (30). The old widower's love for Crisele is the result of a blind passion, of the blindness of his misguided and inappropriate passion. His love is a love concerned only with physical possession, with the material control and ownership of Crisele's beauty. It is not Crisele that Rogat desires so much, but her youthful beauty, the striking physical appearance that sets her apart from the rest. Whereas Memnon's love was said to be a "vraye amitié" (true friendship), Rogat's is simply limited to what Crisele represents, to her sheer value as an object, an object that can be viewed and displayed as a material possession. Furthermore, Rogat's passion for the young Crisele is explicitly sexual, since he does not wish to have any more children. In the logic of Camus's tale, Memnon, in the manner of an idealized medieval knight, admires and glorifies Crisele's beauty for its own sake. Rogat, on the other hand, wants to further his own personal satisfaction by marrying the beautiful Crisele. Her beauty will then become his and his alone, and therefore, in his misguided view, his personal status will be enhanced.

Rogat's voluptuous desire for the young Crisele, his surrender to physical pleasure and the lust activated by his eyes, make his second marriage a mockery of the devout ideal of Christian marriage based on mutual love and the negation of sexual pleasure for its own sake. Saint François de Sales, Camus's spiritual teacher and friend, described characters like Rogat "as gluttons whose mind is in the dishes they eat." This alimentary metaphor, recalling the sin of gluttony, is a constant in the devout literature of seventeenth-century France.[9] Rogat's fascination with Crisele's beauty despite his old age and a previous marriage makes him a prime example of a *profanateur du mariage*. In this context, Memnon's love for Crisele is no longer strictly speaking part of the courtly code but instead exemplifies the true conditions for a happy Christian relationship. This point is significant because it constitutes a crucial element in a series of structured details that reveal the motivation underlying the composition of Camus's narrative as well as the manner in which it seeks to set itself apart from the earlier tales of the legend of the eaten heart. Furthermore, in terms of the narrative economy of "Le Coeur mangé," it is absolutely essential that the just marriage between Crisele and Memnon not materialize and that they never consummate their physical relationship. Rogat possesses the body and the outer beauty of Crisele, whereas Memnon shares with her their reciprocal love.

The opposition between Rogat and Memnon, between the old and the young, is thus articulated in terms of sight and vision, in terms of what the naked eye perceives and what is exhibited by and as a body, on the one hand, and the inner beauty and its rewards, on the other. This opposition between the two male protagonists, between what we might call the two modalities of the heart in Camus's narrative, constitutes one of the key factors in his radical dislocation of his narrative from its "original" context, that is, its courtly and pagan context. It also determines the possibility of drawing out a Christian moral from the narrative, a moral grounded in devout theology and spirituality that condemns blind jealousy and the misapplication and abuse of fortune and parental authority. This moral is in clear opposition to the structure of all the tales of the legend of the eaten heart (with the notable exception of Boccaccio's Tancred—but in the story of Tancred, the heart is not eaten). Furthermore, in the earlier versions of the legend, the consummation of the physical relationship between the wife (or daughter, in Tancred's case) and her lover, determines the nature of the woman's mourning after she is informed of the death of her lover.

The mourning that is described in the earlier texts is a "normal" mourning; it occurs after the death of the lover and, in effect, the husband's action aims to inaugurate such a mourning. In this instance, the feeding of the heart functions in a conventional triangular structure in terms of which the figurative system supported by the heart operates the exchange and substitutions between the three protagonists. In this scenario the mourning of the lady is public and effective, since it ultimately leads to the exile of the husband or husbands. In Camus's case there is a double mourning, a doubling of the work of mourning that entails a crucial shift and displacement from the public and communal register to the body proper of Crisele. Thus the unique organization of Camus's text derives its coherence and intelligibility from a different conception of the relations between the body of the woman and mourning, a conception that conceives mourning exclusively in terms of the heart's figurative powers.

In this subtle and surreptitious change introduced by Camus into the narrative of the legend of the eaten heart, we can thus trace a critical displacement of a number of essentially courtly and "pagan" texts whose primary gesture consisted in embedding carnal love in a problematic dominated by the primacy of reciprocity. In the courtly texts, the central theme is the conflict between two loves, between the love of the husband and the love of the wife. In Camus's text, what is at first presented as an effort to depict the effects of marital jealousy and the blindness of Crisele's parents turns out to be the principle by which anthropophagy and its violence are inscribed into a figurative and narrative apparatus organized around the question of mourning, the question of the fragmentary and fragmented tomb and, ultimately, the empty sepulcher. Indeed, in "Le Coeur mangé," this empty sepulcher is twice evacuated: first by Memnon, before his death, and as if to publicize for the last time his ultimate devotion to Crisele, a devotion which negates and opposes the relationship between Crisele and Rogat. After his death, Memnon chooses to represent himself by his heart; he manifests himself in the guise of his detached heart. Once Crisele receives the heart of her dead lover, she proceeds to bury it in a tomb. The heart replaces the body of the lover in this initial tomb; it displaces the potential but negated physical relations between the two young lovers into a structure that once again excludes Rogat. The husband's revenge, his emptying the tomb of the heart and the introduction of the heart, under the disguise of food, into the body of his wife, makes possible what was strictly forbidden, actualizing what was impossible in life. This second tomb, literally Crisele's stomach, activates in public for the first and last time the secret identification and union of the two bodies.

The realization of this otherwise impossible union produces the effect of a return of mourning, of its inflection and interiorization inside the female body. In other words, the heart, once eaten and digested by the desired body, is in effect reborn, recreated, and regenerated. Not only is the heart of the dead lover reborn, but Crisele regains temporarily her vitality and freedom. After her marriage to Rogat, Crisele "was forced to leave what she loved more than life, to embrace a man she hated more than death. She nonetheless resolved by effort of extraordinary virtue to sacrifice herself to obedience and to leave the chains of gold to burden herself with chains of iron" (34–35). The feeding of the heart and the revelation of the husband's cruelty lead Crisele finally to liberate herself from her imposed prison by informing a relative of Memnon "who was the depository of his heart" (42) of Rogat's actions. The relative then kills Rogat in a duel.

Crisele's mourning can thus be divided into two distinct stages. The first one accompanies the burial of Memnon's heart and Crisele's public devotion to its sepulcher. This first instance of mourning is performative, consisting of the public display of her mourning, a display that advertises her love for Memnon and thus negates her feeling true love for her husband. The second stage is initiated by Rogat himself in order to put an end to the first one. The heart, transformed and disguised as food for Crisele's body, reduced to a body that is merely food, reproduces the dead lover, in his desire, in the effects of his desire inside of the woman he desires. This second instance will result at the end of the narrative in another form of mourning that rehearses the sad story of the two young lovers: "The ties of Crisele are thus broken; she flings herself into a cloister where she lives out her life mourning her faults and always nourishing in her soul the memory of the cruelty of her parents and the friendship of Memnon, able to say with the Queen of Carthage as described by the greatest of the Roman poets: he who had my first affections carried them with him into the sepulcher" (42–43).

The passage from the first to the second phase of mourning creates a change in the status of mourning itself and leads to a reorientation and crystallization of the desire of the woman, a desire that now names a victim and demands vengeance and justice. The active deployment of Crisele's mourning, her demand for action, revives, once and for all, the dead Memnon. It revives his memory in the violated and transfigured body that now hosts his deformed heart. It regenerates the desires of the dead Memnon from within the body that can no longer be its sepulcher because it has been violated and transfigured, because the heart of the dead Memnon has been dissolved and digested. This transfiguration of the body and the heart it hosts highlights the centrality of the heart as the engine and support for the multiple representations of the dead and their survival.

The first sepulcher was symbolically empty. The body of the lover was missing; it was only present through his heart. The second sepulcher, Crisele's own body, is also empty. It is only an intermediary, a passage, a figure of a sepulcher, for eating amounts to burying food in the stomach and transforming that food into the indispensable nourishment for the life of the body. Constructing a sepulcher amounts to hiding the corpse and its ephemeral nature, covering it up, maintaining its death through an image and a figure of its memory and survival. Rogat's violation of the sepulcher stems from his desire to collapse the two practices into a single event. He seeks to eliminate Memnon's heart as the active trace of his relationship with Crisele both by destroying its public sepulcher and by denying it any other permanent status. Rogat tries to dispel Memnon's shadow, his haunting phantom, by violently destroying his last remnant and denying his heart a resting place. He ultimately tries to complete Memnon's burial by transferring his heart into the body of Crisele.

Rogat's initial reaction to his wife's devotion to her dead lover, to his sepulcher and his survival through its powers of representation, is to assume that the news of Memnon's death is simply a ruse and a lie:[10] "The so-frequent visits that Crisele made to the sepulcher, the disdain she had for her appearance, dressing only as if she were in mourning, were like so many hammer blows on the head of our old man, such that his whole imagination served only to raise in his mind that furious transport called jealousy. He got it into his head that perhaps the news of Memnon's death was false and that his wife, visiting him secretly rather than visiting his tomb, was covering her treason with a feigned appearance and a hypocritical sacrilege" (39–40). Rogat's confusion between the actual grief of his wife and its fictional possibility highlights the interplay between the literal and the figurative so dominant in the narrative. Crisele's mourning, the way she dresses, because of her marital status represents a fictional mourning ("dressing only *as if* in mourning"). Corresponding to this dangerous fiction is another one, the one inscribed on the sepulcher itself ("to give the memory of Memnon an image of life"). Between the fictional, figurative representation of the survival of the dead and the real and perceived mourning of Crisele, Rogat's status as husband is undermined and effectively erased. His suspicion of Crisele's betrayal, through its phantasmagoric effects, leads him to kill the remnants of the dead as if to ensure the death of Memnon. This double violence inflicted on the dead Memnon, or on what is left of him and what he has left behind to Crisele, constitutes the major transgression described in Camus's tale. The feeding of the heart thus becomes Rogat's only means of ensuring the authenticity of the death of Memnon and the negation of his symbolic survival.

The feeding of the heart, however, reanimates Crisele's passion and, in a sense, reactivates the dead Memnon. By emptying the tomb and transferring its contents into the body of Crisele, Rogat inadvertently gives body to the heart of the dead Memnon. He gives it the body it has always desired, the body in which it becomes invisible but also alive again. The transfiguration of the heart, brought about through the active mediation of food, displays the paradoxical powers of the revival of the dead in the body of the living and its desire for survival as pure desire. The feeding of the heart dramatically changes Crisele's attitude toward Rogat and the death of Memnon. Instead of her initial passive reaction and submission to her fate, she now seeks vengeance. It is as if, thanks to the incorporated heart of her dead lover, Crisele has become an other—it is as if she has also become Memnon himself. Thus, Crisele "excited the relative of Memnon so much to vengeance that he challenged the old man to a duel, and he made him vomit his cruel and jealous soul with his blood" (42). Here we see the ultimate impact of Rogat's perverse revenge. If, in the opening lines of the tale, Camus introduced his story as that of the war waged by the living on the dead, we might now say that the conclusion of "Le Coeur mangé" culminates in the triumph of the dead in the war they wage on the living. Memnon's heart, once introduced into the body of Crisele, activates a chain reaction that leads to Rogat's death. And Rogat's death is described as the exact opposite of Memnon's second death, which becomes a resurrection. Rogat is made to vomit his soul, whereas Memnon's heart was eaten by Crisele. Rogat's death echoes Memnon's double death because it combines the military dimension mentioned earlier with a figurative homologue to the feeding of the heart to Crisele.

"Spectacles of Horror"

The closure of Camus's narrative, its perfect recapitulation of the original act of violence, and the valorization of the privileged relationship between Crisele and Memnon invite another reading, one that highlights the connotations and semantic richness of the names of the three main protagonists of the narrative. In Camus's tale, the names of the three principal protagonists display a fundamentally different order of referentiality from the one we have encountered in the earlier texts of the legend. Indeed, they open up the text to a larger and problematic reference that will lead us to the theological subtext that guides and informs the organization of "Le coeur mangé." In one of the Boccaccio stories, the story of the two Guillaumes, the names of the two knights disputing the love of the lady were almost identical except for a qualifier, a marker of space and identity that also served to highlight their geographical proximity and their interchangeability. The two Guillaumes are characterized and distinguished by their feudal domain, by the name of their territory and the space in which they exert their power without any opposition. The story of their mutual friendship and its perversion into mortal hatred emphasizes their similar status and the possibility of substitution between the two domains their names represent. In "Le Coeur mangé," on the other hand, the names will allow us to follow the theological inspiration of the tale to its end.

Memnon's name takes us to Homer's *Iliad* and Virgil's *Aeneid*.[11] In Virgil, Memnon, the son of the king of Ethiopia, ally of the Trojans and slain by Achilles, symbolizes friendship and sacrifice. It is perhaps no coincidence that Memnon's name appears in the *Aeneid* immediately after the scene depicting the Trojan women in their mourning procession. The *Aeneid* is referred to explicitly at the end of "Le Coeur mangé," where Crisele is identified with Dido: "Crisele . . . who could say like this Queen of Carthage as described by the greatest of Roman poets: he who had my first affections carried them with him into the sepulcher" (43).[12] After his death on the field of battle, and in recognition of his qualities, Memnon was made immortal by Zeus. Memnon's immortality, his symbolic passage from the mortality of men, through battle, to the ranks of the immortals, reinforces the Christian, theological, and allegorical dimension of Camus's text. Memnon's death as a man and his resurrection as an immortal clearly mark him as a figure who is identified with Jesus Christ.

Crisele's name, on the other hand, appears to derive from Griselda or Griselde, the famous wife and queen immortalized by Boccaccio and others for her loyalty and patience.[13] In Camus's text, Crisele's name defines and describes her actions, her unfailing loyalty and devotion to her lover. Whereas the legendary Griselde was renowned for her patience and loyalty to her husband, Camus's Crisele devotes herself to her lover. This is a significant detail, for in terms of the theological framework of the narrative, it is crucial that Crisele and Memnon not be married.

Rogat's name is the most interesting and problematic of the three and also the most difficult to fit into the scheme of the narrative. Its origin is uncertain, but it may be related to Rogatien, a saint and martyr, who was killed with his brother Donatien around 299 A.D. Before his death Rogatien was jailed and tortured, and he was beheaded. Another possible source for the name is the Rogations, the ceremonies celebrated before Ascension. According to Gregory of Tours, the Rogations were first instituted by Saint Avitus:

> In the Homily which Saint Avitus composed on the Rogations he says that these ceremonies, which we celebrate before the triumph of our lord's Ascension, were instituted by Mamertus, Bishop of that same town of Vienne of which Avitus held the episcopate when he was writing, at a time when the townsfolk were terrified by a series of portents. Vienne was shaken by frequent earthquakes, and savage packs of wolves and stags came in through the gates and ranged through the entire city, fearing nothing and nobody, or so he writes. These portents continued throughout the whole year. As the season of the feast of Easter approached, the common people in their devotion expected God's compassion on them, hoping that this day of great solemnity might see an end to their terror. However, on the very vigil of the holy night, when the rite of Mass was being celebrated, the King's palace inside the city walls was set ablaze by fire sent by God. The congregation was panic-stricken. They rushed out of the church, for they thought that the whole town would be destroyed by this fire, or else that the earth would open and swallow it up. The holy Bishop was prostrate before the altar, imploring God's mercy with tears and lamentations. What

more should I say? The prayers of this famous Bishop rose to heaven and, so to speak, his floods of tears put out the fire in the palace. While this was going on, the feast of the Ascension of our Lord was coming nearer, as I have told you. Mamertus told the people to fast, he instituted a special form of prayer, a religious service and a grant of alms to the poor in thanksgiving. All the horrors came to an end. The story of what had happened spread through all the provinces and led all the bishops to copy what this particular prelate had done in faith. Down to our times these rites are celebrated with a contrite spirit and a grateful heart in all of our churches to the glory of God.[14]

The names of the actors in Camus's "spectacle of horror" display the structural principle regulating the organization of the narrative. At the center of this structure lies the heart, the most important and powerful vehicle of representation. The heart constitutes the convergence of figurative and metaphorical structures on the locus of the central bodily function that is itself represented as an extension and the principle of the living body. The heart is the kernel of an apparatus of exchange and substitutions centered around the possibilities of the representation of the body, of the dead and the living body, and the presentation of that representation in discourse. Between the body and discourse, as in the space separating the dead from the living, the heart traces and marks the insurmountable boundaries as well as the troubling zones of interference and intersection between the two. The "heart" of the story of "Le Coeur mangé" is precisely this eaten and assimilated heart, this hidden and surviving heart in all its transformations and displacements. Underlying the figurative deployment of the violent and mysterious story of this heart is another mystery and another secret, those of naming and reproducing, through specific rhetorical strategies, an inaccessible heart, a heart that is the mystery par excellence as the source and the foundation of the narrative of the eaten heart.

Camus's story, identifying its subject matter in its own movement, eats the "heart," so to speak, in its narration, in its impulse
to narrate and represent its story under the guise of the presentation of an act of perverse feeding. The sympathies of the reader
are obviously with Crisele and her lover, and thus the reader is
also subjected to a similar violence, a similar surreptitious feeding.
In terms of this double register, the conclusion of the story puts
forth its secret and driving desire in the words of the force-feeder,
the husband. In the same manner in which Rogat secretly feeds
his wife the heart of her dead lover, Camus's narrative seeks to
feed the reader secret words, secret names, through the story of
Crisele and Memnon that, once assimilated, will reveal the full
power and the intimate relations between feeding and reading,
between eating or devouring and writing. The devoured word,
disguised in a representation, very much like the heart, will
contaminate the body and will lead to a form of rejection or
"throwing out."

What Crisele, in the specific terms of the tale, throws out is
Rogat's soul, or, more precisely, the words that lead to his
throwing out his soul, his claim over her body. The final act in
the narrative consecrates Crisele's perverse physical union with
her dead lover and her final liberation from marriage and Rogat.
In a similar fashion, the reader of the story is led to resist reading
as a form of incorporation, as a form of interiorization of an alien
body. This exteriority of reading preserves the status of the text
as other, as ultimately inaccessible. The ultimate gesture of this
text, its great phantasmagoric obsession, is a gesture of nostalgia,
a nostalgia devoted to mourning a fundamental loss, an incom-
plete correspondence between words and food, between names
and events. Camus's text is motivated by a secret design, a desire
to reenact a mystery, the Christian mystery par excellence. This
impossible dream of the narrative gives rise to an elaborate and
surreptitious identification with the narrative of the mystery that

"Le Coeur mangé" aims to reenact and rehearse. Since that other narrative is a mystery, since it is itself a secret that haunts Camus's narrative, it cannot be named or identified directly. It can only be designated by a secret name, a name that is known only to the initiate. And this name is uttered by the force-feeder: "But Crisele wishing to continue her visits and devotions to the tomb of the heart of Memnon, Rogat one day said to her that she didn't need to take so much trouble since she was carrying this tomb everywhere in her own stomach, like another Artemisia serving as sepulcher to the heart of her lover" (41–42).

The Christianization of Pagan Mourning

Artemisia, the queen of Caria, who succeeded her husband and brother to the throne and was said to have swallowed the ashes of her husband mixed with wine, is named by Rogat as Crisele's model. Indeed, Artemisia devoted her life to mourning her dead husband, building in his memory the famous Mausoleum that was considered one of the seven wonders of the world. Artemisia is the paradigm for mourning, for the everlasting grief over the loss of the loved person.

Cicero has an interesting discussion of Artemisia in his *Tusculanarum Disputationum*:

> It has, I think, been sufficiently insisted on that distress is the idea of a present evil with this implication in it, that it is a duty to feel distress.
>
> An addition to this definition is rightly made by Zeno, namely that this idea of a present evil is a "fresh" one [*ut illa opinio praesentis mali sit recens*]. This word, however, his followers interpret to mean that not only, according to their view, is that "fresh" which has taken place a short time previously, but that so long as the imagined evil preserves a certain power of being vigorous and retaining so to speak its greenness [*viriditatem*], it is termed

"fresh." For instance, the famous Artemisia, wife of Mausolus, King of Caria, who built the celebrated burial monument at Halicarnassus, lived in sorrow all her days and wasted away under its enfeebling influence. The idea of her sorrow was "fresh" for her every day, and this idea only ceases to be termed "fresh" when it has withered away by length of time. These therefore are the duties of comforters: to do away with distress root and branch, or allay it, or diminish it as far as possible, or stop its progress and not allow it to extend further, or to divert it elsewhere.[15]

Cicero's discussion centers around the temporality of mourning, of the "freshness" of grief. In the case of Artemisia, that "freshness" was never tarnished by time. She lived her life from the position of her mourning. Crisele, in Camus's story, lives her life from the position and the perspective of her dead lover, even more so when she has his heart in her stomach. The literal incorporation of the heart or a part of the body of the lover into the body of the woman transforms the woman and makes her a vehicle for the dead. Thus, both Artemisia and Crisele negate the future, deny its possibility without the existence and the company of the dead lover. They both live in a fixed present, a present that is always a past-present, an impossible and imaginary present that cannot forget what it experiences as an irredeemable loss. This past-present is not the past remembered, the past reconstructed and recreated in its fullness. It is, instead, a recreation of an illusory past in the present, the invention of a utopian time where the dead still act after their deaths. This past-present is utterly inadmissible, violent, and threatening, and thus receives its most significant manifestation in a monumentalization of the memory of the loss and the lost. The temporality of mourning exemplified by Artemisia is a lived temporality, lived with and from the position of the dead, of the dead living in representation, in the representation of that memory as a public monument or a complete and total withdrawal from the public domain. The "freshness" of mourning ultimately consists in the approximation of the evacuation of a single and unique moment in time, its crystallization and fixation as both the moment of death and the life after death.

In its double movement, here illustrated by the identification of Artemisia and Crisele, the structure of this temporality brings to the surface the main motivation of Camus's narrative. It finally names, under the guise of another name and another set of associations, the guiding principle informing the details of "Le Coeur mangé." The double death of Memnon, the emptying of his sepulcher, the devotion of Crisele and her withdrawal to a convent after the death of Rogat, are all signs that point to Camus's desire to tell the Christian story par excellence, the story of the death of Christ and his resurrection, within the general structure of the legend of the eaten heart. The empty sepulcher recalls the empty sepulcher of Christ, and Rogat's name, closely identified with the days separating the death of Christ on the cross and his resurrection, names the other two protagonists of the narrative in mystical and spiritual terms.

The appearance of Artemisia as the model for Crisele's experience emphasizes the loss of the body of the lover, or at least its most important representative, the heart. What Camus perceives as the intimate relation between his heroine and Artemisia is not their public devotion to their lovers but instead their interiorization of the body of their lover. This detail is significant because it highlights the emptying out of the sepulcher and its transfer to the body of the woman. And it is precisely this empty tomb, through the reference to Artemisia, that brings out the theological subtext informing Camus's narrative. In order to make this subtext more explicit, I will examine Jean de la Ceppède's *Les Théorèmes sur le Sacré Mystère de Notre Rédemption* (Theorems on the Sacred Mystery of Our Redemption), published in three volumes between 1613 and 1622.[16] Camus was familiar with La Ceppède's poetry, and the similarity in their views will become apparent. La Ceppède's *Théorèmes* consist of three hundred sonnets devoted to the life of Christ and accompanied by the most remarkably erudite annotation. In the third book, which recounts the death and resurrection of Christ, we find this sonnet:

> Thus the distraught virgin mourned her hurt,
> Only in the spirit, speaking only with her eyes:
> Building in her heart, for the object of her love, as best she can
> (Like the *Carian*) *a living mausoleum.*
> But her pain can no longer be hidden.
> It moves her heart, and Earth and the Heavens,
> It has to be exhaled through her mouth,
> Her heart thus from her mouth explodes into black adieux.
> "Adieu my Son, through whom Motherhood
> Was once very sweet for me, today very bitter.
> Since I can no longer see your increasing years, I'll die.
> Adieu my sweet care, *my dear food.*
> Adieu my sad emotion, *my living sepulcher.*
> *Adieu to you through whom I had life and through whom I die.*"
> (III, LXII)

In La Ceppède's vision, Artemisia represents the Virgin Mary in her devotion to her dying son. The Greek paradigm of mourning and grief has now been transposed into a strictly Christian problematic, one that relies for its intelligibility on the partial identification of Artemisia and Mary. (This identification is only partial because Mary is a virgin, and her title as the spouse of Christ was only figurative and was never universally received.[17]) In this perspective, Crisele's virginity reinforces her identification with the Virgin. In another sonnet of *Les Théorèmes* that appears at the end of the volume with a number of other poems addressed to La Ceppède and praising his work, the relations between Mary and Artemisia are explained in full detail:

Mausoleus didn't exist, any more than Artemisia
Whom you boast of, Gregeois, so often to their credit,
It is only a vain dream, everything said to us
About this royal tomb, marvelous undertaking.

Mausoleus is the Christ, Artemisia the Church,
Or the peerless Virgin that the Oracle predicted;
The Cross, the Mausoleum where Jesus Christ hung,
To give us by dying our first freedom.

To this royal tomb this faithful wife
For a great prize calls from everywhere,
To praise her husband, the finest minds.

Ceppède is one of the latest come to this project,
But his divine work gives him the advantage
To contest the first for the glory of this prize.[18]

This explanatory poem denies the authenticity of the Greek legend in favor of the figurative and representational power of the story of Artemisia and the manner in which it symbolizes Christ's death and his relation to the Church and the Virgin. Whereas Artemisia voluntarily "incorporated" the body of her dead husband, Crisele was secretly fed the heart of her lover, and Mary constructed, in her heart, a living tomb for her dead son. The passage from the literal to the figurative, from the Greek to the Christian, reinforces the allegorical dimension of the legend of Artemisia and consequently of "Le Coeur mangé." And it is precisely this Christian allegorical problematic that informs Camus's narrative and accounts for the important variation he introduces into the story of the eaten heart. Furthermore, once this theological subtext is identified, various details in the text take on a new significance. As we have seen in the earlier versions of the legend of the eaten heart, the taste of the heart is clearly identified with sexuality and sexual pleasure. In Camus's text, however, Crisele does not express her great pleasure and satisfaction after eating the heart. The only feature or element that attracts her attention is simply the odor of the heart: "He had his cook chop Memnon's heart and make it into a pâté with other meat, and in this way he had Crisele eat it without knowing it. It is true, as it had been embalmed, that she said when eating it that this flesh was perfumed, at which the jealous old man took to laughing, but it was sardonic laughter" (41).[19] In theological terms, the odor of the meat recalls either the odor of the sacrament or the question of whether Christ's body rotted after his death. In either case, Crisele's reaction avoids expressing directly the sexual connotations of the meal.

Another detail concerns the fate of the women after the revelation of the husband's actions. In Boccaccio and the *Roman du châtelain de Couci,* the woman dies either of starvation or of grief and is then buried, in Boccaccio's version, with her lover. In Camus's version, Crisele, after the death of Rogat, retires to a convent. On the face of it, this is a conventional conclusion. Yet, in theological terms, the convent consecrates the virginity of the woman and her symbolic marriage to Christ, two elements that reinforce my interpretation of the allegorical dimension of Camus's text. Furthermore, the convent, in ecclesiastical literature— a literature with which Camus was more than familiar—is described as the tomb of the woman. Here is a passage from the *Regula monacharum* found in Saint Jerome's works: "On account of this, dearest one, let your convent be your tomb: where you will be dead and buried with Christ, until rising with Him you will appear in His glory. Finally, the thing that is most frightening to the one lying in a burial mound is the grave robber who sneaks in at night to steal precious treasure. Thieves dig this up, to steal with infinite skill the treasure that is inside. Therefore the tomb is watched over by a bishop whom God installed as the primary guardian in His vineyard. It is guarded by a resident

*The Virgin, Saint John, Saint Sebastien, and
Saint Roch adoring the Sacred Heart.*

priest who discharges his duty on the premises: so that no one enters recklessly nor that anyone tries to weaken the tomb."[20]

The phantasmagoric structure of Camus's text is here translated into a metaphor for virginity and sexuality. The treasure buried in the tomb, the virginity of the nun and her death in the convent, echo the buried heart and the crypt it gave rise to. In this context, Rogat, the husband, is the equivalent of the thief, the robber who sneaks in to steal away the precious treasure. Indeed, it is clear early on that Rogat, in the words of the text, married a dead woman: "She nevertheless protested to him [Memnon], and even made no hestitation to declare to her parents and to Rogat as well, that her heart would always be where she had rested her first affection, and that *the old man would have of her nothing but a body without a soul, a body that would nonetheless be chaste and faithful until death*" (36). Rogat is thus ultimately denied any possession of his wife, who remains chaste until her death.

Camus's "Le Coeur mangé," in the manner in which it recapitulates a mythological and narrative tradition that it then inscribes in a devout and mystical theological context, provides us with a unique instance in the long tradition of the legend of the eaten heart. The narrative leads to a closure of the "traditional" form of mourning, the mourning we encountered in the *Lai d'Ignaure,* in the *Roman du châtelain de Couci,* and in Boccaccio. At the same time and in the same gesture, it puts forth the death of Memnon and his symbolic reanimation as a paradigm for an affective organization of a larger structure, a structure founded and dedicated to a search for what has mysteriously disappeared. The theological allegory we have uncovered in Camus's text demonstrates that for the devout tradition of the seventeenth century in France, the founding moment of the mystical quest for the reunion with the divine is located in the experience of the loss and absence of the body of Christ and its offering as a ritualized sacrifice. In this context, Crisele's retreat to the convent represents a significant transformation of the Greek Artemisia. Whereas Artemisia, in order to preserve the active memory and presence of her dead husband, interiorizes the ashes of his body into her own and thus monumentalizes his death and her devotion to his memory, Crisele joins a monument that symbolizes her public death, her withdrawal from the world, and her consecration to the memory of Christ when she retires to the world of the convent.

This transformation of Artemisia reveals the fundamental differences between the Greek and Christian traditions regarding their conception and representation of death and the ways in which they remember the dead. Crisele's entry into the convent, in spiritual terms, constitutes a new beginning, a new life and new possibilities founded on the promised return of the dead and the eventual reunion with Christ. In terms of the theology that informs the structure of Camus's tale, the act of eating human flesh, cannibalism itself, is transformed and translated into a new order in the same way that the Eucharist closes and recapitulates the original sin occasioned by the eating of the apple. Such a transformation is inaugurated by the actions of Rogat, whose name recalls the sacrifice and resurrection of Christ and thus inscribes the translation of anthropophagy into Christianity's magical metaphor of food becoming a body, an edible body. This transfiguration of the "pagan" and courtly antecedents of the legend of the eaten heart is announced by Camus in his preface to the *Spectacles d'horreur:* "If you are one of those timid Israelites, reader, who didn't have the courage to cross the Red Sea because the blood-colored waves horrified them, go no further in reading this book, which will show you only spectacles of blood and carnage. But if you resemble Caleb and Joshua, who had contempt for those cowardly spies of the promised land who related that that country devoured its inhabitants, and that it was inhabited by cannibals or eaters of men, fear not to open these pages, and to cross this Jordan River" (Preface).[21]

The *Spectacle d'horreur* that is "Le Coeur mangé" is thus to be read in the manner of Caleb and Joshua. Cannibalism is simply a cover and a veil that is there in order to keep away the ones who do not believe. The book itself, full of bloody scenes and tales of death and carnage, if read correctly—that is to say, if read in spiritual and mystical terms—is none other than the story of the promised land itself and of how to gain access to it. And the act of reading in the manner of Caleb and Joshua is equivalent to baptism, the washing of the body in the river Jordan with its regenerative and redemptive powers. Thus the secret of this text appears to be the secret of Christianity itself, the secret of life and death and of life after death. What haunts "Le Coeur mangé" is the mystery that cannot be named directly, the mystery that can only be constructed and given significance in the words and terms of what it seeks to negate. The allegory of reading that was for Camus the allegory that annihilates and destroys, by literally swallowing and digesting the constitutive words, the stories of the allegories of the heart and its eating, becomes the active gesture of eating the mystical body of Christ in its impossible textual description, its impossible emergence into the discursive and narrative order of representation.

FOUR

Elephantine Marriage and Devout Sexuality

Then came the great elephant . . . the wise elephant, that is
our Lord Jesus Christ.

BRITISH MUSEUM *BESTIARY*[1]

Camus's "Le Coeur mangé" brings out the devout and mystical
dimensions of the legend of the eaten heart. By doing so, it
reveals the ways in which the Devout discourse of the early
seventeenth century in France tried to combat and respond to
the rising popularity of the narrative form and the proliferation
of short stories and romance novels. It is revealing to examine
some of the founding texts of the Devout tradition and to
investigate the manner in which they exploited the relations
between food and the discussion and representation of sexuality.
Such a detour will inevitably lead us to the writings of Saint
François de Sales and his efforts to bring mysticism to the masses.

Before the apogee of the Moralist tradition and its radical
critique of the grounding of subjectivity in the representations of
self-love, the analysis of passions in the first half of the seventeenth
century was concentrated on the development of an ethical dis-

{103}

course of love as the foundation of a Christian pragmatics. This ethical drive is most apparent in the construction and organization of a work like Senault's *De l'Usage des passions* (1641). A major and unfortunately often neglected tradition behind this pragmatic ethics finds its most significant and polished expression in the two central works of Saint François de Sales. Between the *Introduction à la vie dévote* (Introduction to Devout Life, 1608) and the *Traité de l'amour de Dieu* (Treatise on the Love of God, 1616), we find a remarkable distillation of the ideal of Devout life in all its ramifications, a life that is by definition and in principle never fully detached from the complex demands and necessities of everyday life.[2] Instead of recommending a rigid and facile withdrawal from the daily matters of life, Saint François tries to define a new and complete "devout" life that will eventually absorb and replace the everyday life. Thus we find in his corpus an elaborate and detailed descriptive analysis of the modalities of the events constituting daily life, grounded and informed by the ideal of mystical devotion and the desire for an unmediated union with God.

Theology and Perverse Sexuality

As one might expect, at the center of this "devout" daily life lies the crucial and inescapable question of sexuality and sexual practice. In fact, we encounter the most prescriptive passages of the *Introduction à la vie dévote* in the chapters devoted to the discussions of sexuality. For, in the "devout" life as understood and defined by Saint François, sexuality resides outside the norm and the normal, and yet it represents the most difficult and inevitable subject for a "devout" pragmatics of everyday life. Celibacy, the monastic norm, constitutes the utopian ideal behind the efforts to contain and to minimize the presence of sexuality in daily life. This desire to neutralize sexuality—for indeed we are faced in the

Devout ethical discourse with a desire with its own economy and drives—accounts for the specificity of the figurative mythology and strategy deployed in order to produce a valid or persuasive representation of the inherent perversity of the most benign sexual practices. This "desired" representation relies, for its coherence and intelligibility, on the conflation and confrontation of a double origin. The first component of this double origin is derived from the general cultural norm and the accepted rules of etiquette and protocol; the second component stems from the direct imposition of a specific theological interpretation of the cultural norm itself. In other words, the theological framework is used here as a tool for selection and presentation that makes possible the representation of sexuality under the guise of distorted and perverted basic cultural practices. With the same gesture, the selected cultural practice highlights and problematizes the theological discourse, conceived and given as its sole source of intelligibility. In other words, Saint François's texts play out the conflicts between theology reduced to a simplified set of practical guidelines and the forces, social and other, driving daily life.

In order to illustrate this Devout economy of desire, I will discuss some representative passages from the *Introduction à la vie dévote* and the *Traité de l'amour de Dieu*. In the chapter of the former work entitled "De l'Honnêteté du lit nuptial" (The Sanctity of the Marriage Bed), Saint François discusses most explicitly the general question or problem of sexual desire. His discussion, however, proceeds from a basic and fundamental analogy: "There is a certain resemblance between sexual pleasures and those taken in eating. Both of them are related to the flesh but because of their animal vehemence the first are called carnal pleasures without qualification."[3] Eating and sexuality are equated and named as identical for, in the rest of the chapter, the "certain resemblance" proves to be a total and perfect resemblance on the basis of the highly charged term "flesh." Between taking in food and desiring the other under the only normal circumstances recognized by the Church, namely marriage, between the pleasures of the table and the pleasures of the bed, Saint François elaborates and develops the codes of Devout behavior. The articulation of these codes proceeds from an impossibility, from a desire not to name sexual pleasure directly because its naming carries the inevitable elements of its inherent dangerous perversity: "I will try to explain what I cannot say about sexual pleasure by what I say of the (pleasures of eating)" (226). The identification at the basis of the condemnation of sexual pleasures is first and foremost a requirement of intelligibility, for by its negation and denegation it names and presents what is radically unnameable and absent from the Devout order of everyday life. With this negative modality of representation firmly in place, the Devout ethical discourse proceeds uninhibited:

> Honorable people think of the table only as they sit down, and after the meal they wash their hands and mouths so as to no longer experience the taste and odor of what they have eaten. The elephant is only a huge beast, but he is the most worthy that lives on the earth and has the most sense. I want to tell you about a characteristic of his honesty: he never changes females and loves tenderly the one he has chosen, with whom he nonetheless copulates only every three years, and that only for five days, so secretly that he is never seen in the act. But he is seen, however, on the sixth day, on which, before doing anything else, he goes straight to some river in which he washes his whole body, wishing in no way to return to the herd before he is purified. Are these not beautiful and honest feelings on the part of such an animal, who in so doing invites married people to disengage their affections from the sensuality and voluptuousness in which, because of their (married) state, they

will have engaged, but these over, (they are to) wash their hearts and affections of them and to purify themselves of them as soon as possible.[4] (228–229)

The elephant is put forward here as the indisputable paradigm of "honnêteté" and civilized behavior. Its comportment exemplifies the desired norm of "devout life" by emphasizing a general sense of sociability associated with loyalty and faithfulness at the expense of sexual desire. The human equivalent of this idealized elephantine behavior is none other than good table manners, marked and determined by cleanliness and immediacy. Indeed, the first aim of the paradigmatic element and its association with food and table manners as a representation of sexual desire is to devalorize and condemn the unmediated nature of desire itself. It is as if sexuality in the Devout order of things can be reduced to a recurrent order, a low-frequency sequence, thus reducing it to a naturalized cyclical activity. The elephantine cycle, in Saint François's text, eliminates all public display of the pleasures associated with sexuality by reducing it to a mere antisocial performance. "It is an infallible mark of a wayward, infamous, base, abject, and degraded mind to think about food and drink before mealtime, much more so to delight in ourselves later with the pleasure we had in eating, keeping it alive in words and imagination and taking delight in recalling the sensual satisfaction we had in swallowing those bits of food" (228). The sexual act, modeled on the Devout table manners, lies outside the social order and is to be kept there. And, in this context, the elephantine cycle is highly suggestive: it takes place once every three years and for a period of five days, the sixth day being reserved for the necessary cleansing process. Thus the elephant mates in secrecy and resurfaces into society only after having erased the marks of its sexual desire. Yet the numerology of the elephantine cycle recalls all too easily the numerology of the narrative of creation in the book of Genesis and its Christian companion, the trinity. Sexuality, in the Christian doctrine, is the direct result of the Fall and as such reenacts the separation of man from his creator in the form of sexual union. Furthermore, the Fall itself follows from a seduction and a desire fulfilled through an act of transgressive eating, and thus eating and table manners constitute a logical and legitimate figure, in the Devout tradition, for sexual desire.

Genesis describes the eating of the apple in terms of excess and surplus, in terms of moral delectation in the unnecessary and the superfluous. This "excessive" quality of original sin is echoed in the Christian and Devout discourse on sexuality in particular and the passions in general through the perfect correspondence between sexuality and gluttony. The equivalence between these two forms of excess is spelled out in a book on marriage inspired directly by the writings of Saint François de Sales. The full title of the 1683 anonymous manual is *Instructions on Marriage in the Form of a Dialogue between a Mother and her Daughter. In which the Ceremonies of this Sacrament are Explained, with the Mysteries that it Holds and the Holiness with which Christians Should Enter into it and Live.* Here is a representative passage describing the dangers of gluttony and bad table manners as a figure for sexual desire:

> *Pauline:* By what signs can one know if one is one of these wretches?
>
> *Paule:* When, at table, one focuses wholly on the voluptuousness of drinking and eating, and is as if plunged and absorbed in it, the mind incapable of thinking with liberty about any other thing. For there are people whose souls are so buried in the sensation of their brutish affection, that they are even incapable of reflecting on and distinguishing those very things that cause voluptuousness, as they are like someone in an ecstasy, if I can use this term to express the

force of their brutish affection . . . What I have said about gluttony, my dear daughter, you must apply to marriage procedures. I could not with decency explain myself in any other way.[5]

In this practical manual intended for the general public we find the full and direct application of the Devout ethics and its representations of sexual desire. Yet I believe it would be a mistake to see in this fundamental figurative strategy simply a convenient and conventional discourse. For the theological imperative at the basis of the identification of sexuality and uncontrolled desire for food necessitates another, more complex and more interesting figurative structure. The devalorization of sexual desire and gluttony leads necessarily, in the logic of Christianity, and in particular in the logic of the Devout ethics elaborated by Saint François de Sales, to the valorization of another form of eating. Already in Saint François's own texts we encounter the return to and the rehabilitation of the culinary figure in its most classical and extreme form. In order to describe the ultimate goal of Devout life and practice, namely "quiétude," Saint François invokes eating as his central and guiding metaphor: "Now, in all these divine mysteries, which include all the others, there is plenty to eat and drink well . . . Now, to eat is to meditate, for in meditating one chews, turning hither and thither the spiritual meat between the teeth of consideration in order to chop it up, abrade it and digest it, which is not done without some effort. To drink is to contemplate and this is done without difficulty or resistance, with pleasure and fluently; but to become drunk is to contemplate so often and so ardently, that one is wholly outside of oneself in order to be wholly in God."[6]

Eating and drinking, in this instance, are no longer the subjects of condemnation. Instead they provide the basis and path for inner transformation and liberation on the way to the mystical union with God the creator. The pleasures associated with eating and drinking name, in this context, the practice of meditation, namely the annihilation of the self, and its ecstasy. We have now fully traversed the distance separating the pleasures of the table as an occasion for the condemnation of the pleasures of the bed to the pleasures of eating as the celebration of the end and finality of Devout life.

   The foundation for this critical reversal in the status of the culinary metaphor derives directly from the central place reserved for the Eucharist and its redemptive powers in the Christian tradition. The Eucharist, the magical act of eating the mystical body of Christ, constitutes the only possible and effective closure to the narrative of the Fall precisely because it *is* an act of eating. It is as if the devout Christian's life and salvation are played out between the mythical eating of the apple and the mystical eating of the Eucharist, and in between lies a series of obstacles and temptations, all described or describable in terms of one form of eating or another. The only difference between these two pri-mordial acts of eating—and this difference, as Pascal would say, is infinite—consists in their direction, orientation, and motiva-tion. The eating of the apple names the disastrous effects of the failure to transfer the divine power and knowledge to mankind, whereas the Eucharist reincorporates humanity into its native and original divine body. The perverse pleasure of the apple gives birth to the pleasures of sexual union and culminates in mortality, and the ecstasy of the Eucharist recaptures the lost pleasure of the Creator in his original union with his creation. The inherent tension in this essentially narrative structure accounts for the apologetic tone and nature of the Devout discourse on sexuality through the intermediary of food, for the Eucharist is animated by a nostalgic vocation and a drive to reproduce, after the fact, the desire and the pleasure dissipated by the Creator at the expense of his creation. The ideal of Devout "honnêteté," or decency, is no more than a cunning ruse and an artificial disguise for the desired expenditure of drives concentrated on the quest for the unmediated reunion with God.

The teleology of Devout ethics defines the body as the locus of the decay and degeneration inaugurated with the Fall. Meditation and contemplation operate the inner transformation and transfiguration of the body and that which it contains in order to render it an acceptable host that desires and receives the divine presence. Indeed, in the mystical tradition underlying the seventeenth-century Devout ethics, the word of God and particularly the ritual celebration of the Eucharist form the process through which the elements of decay and degeneration are regenerated. The terms most frequently used to describe the transformative powers of this Word are, not surprisingly, primarily culinary:

> In effect, the divine word is a salutary water of knowledge, following this word of our Lord: "You are all made clean through the words that I say to you" (John 15). The divine word cooks again, so to speak, the raw thoughts of the flesh in the fire of the Holy Spirit, and changes them into spiritual sentiments, into a food healthy for the soul; so much so that you can truly say: "My heart is heated inside of me, and the fire will light in my meditation."[7]

The redemptive powers of the Eucharist follow exactly the process and the path of transfiguration of the bread and wine into the blood and body of Christ. Furthermore, the practice of meditation works to reproduce the effects of the Eucharist by transforming the "raw thoughts about the flesh" into the "nourishment" of the mystical soul. Since an original act of eating contaminated the body, since in effect it named the body as the locus of contamination, meditation and contemplation, that is to say the practical rehabilitation of the body to its now lost originary, pure status, are, by definition and in principle, conceived of as instances of eating as well. Meditation and contemplation are indeed a culinary exercise, and the practice of meditation and contemplation is, in a manner of speaking, a practice of eating and drinking with its specific table manners and recipes.

The elephant, we recall, was singled out as the model of Devout behavior primarily because of its low sexual appetite and its abhorrence of any recognizable sign or mark of sexual desire. As such, it occupies a privileged position in the Devout bestiary of Saint François de Sales. At the bottom of the scale, we find another problematic animal that condenses the two opposite components of the figuration of eating in the Devout discourse. This innocent and special animal is the butterfly. In the chapter of the *Introduction à la vie dévote* devoted to the necessity of chastity, Saint François offers the butterfly as the image of the individual who cannot resist the temptations of the body:

> As the great Saint Jerome said, the enemy presses virgins violently with the desire for the experience of voluptuousness, representing it as infinitely more pleasant and delicious than it is . . . For, just as the little butterfly who sees the flame flies curiously around it to see if it is as sweet as it is beautiful, and impelled by this fantasy ceases not until it is lost in its first try, so young people all too often allow themselves to be seized by the false and foolish regard that they have for the flames of voluptuousness, so that after several thoughts they will in the end ruin and lose themselves in it.[8] (157)

The butterfly, in the Devout bestiary, constitutes the absolute other of the elephant. Yet there is a well-established topos in the mystical literature in which the butterfly represents the mystical desire itself: "There is in God an immensely deep flame: the heart nonetheless should not fear to touch this adorable flame or to be touched by it; it will not at all be consumed by this so sweet fire, whose tranquil and peaceful heat creates the liaison, harmony and duration of the world."[9] The butterfly, in its double figuration, names the tension if not the contradiction at the heart of the Devout exploitation of the identification of sexuality with

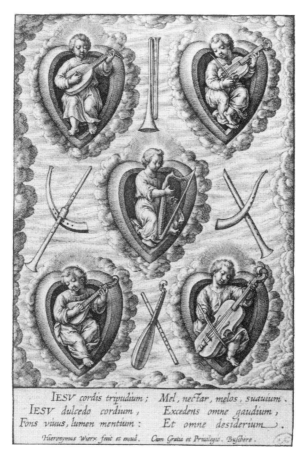

*Christ as a child and a musician
enchanting man's heart.*

eating and table manners. In this instance, it is the image of the flame that names both the seduction of the body and the quest for the reunion with the divinity. This tension at the core of the Devout ethical discourse, if taken literally, produces a suggestive and fascinating, and at the same time perverse, discourse on eating and its theological dimensions. We encounter such a literal interpretation in the writings of Etienne Binet in the first half of the seventeenth century. Binet, an erudite Jesuit, is the author of a number of texts, most of them devoted to the peculiar and the marvelous. The text that is of particular relevance here was published in Paris in 1631; its full title is *Des Attraits tout puissants de l'amour de JESUS-CHRIST, et du Paradis de ce monde* (Concerning the all-powerful appeal of Jesus Christ's love, and of Paradise of this world).[10]

As its title indicates, this book gives a highly rhetorical description of the esoteric and magical powers of Christ through a detailed exposition and analysis of his miracles. The central argument of the book consists in identifying "the most delicate and precious morsel that ever existed in the world."[11] In order to establish Christ's body in the instance of the Eucharist as such an object, Binet gives his reader a fascinating list of competing objects:

> Some say that it was Cleopatra who ate it when she swallowed a pearl worth more than two hundred fifty thousand écus with a sip of vinegar. Others say it was that greedy emperor who ate the Phoenix, or who was made to believe that he had eaten it for his dinner. Some would have it be Queen Artemisia, who pulverized the dead body of King Mausoleus, her lord and husband and, mixing the beloved ashes with wine in a golden cup, swallowed them, and proved better than anyone in the world the truth of these words: *They were two in one flesh.* Others would say it was Adam eating the apple to which was attached the knowledge of good and evil. In short, [others] would have it be this meat, called

that of the twelve divinities who seemed to have imbued it with all
the delicacy of heaven; or finally manna, which is the bread of
heaven and the delight of the Angels. But all this is only a fable or
figure representing the meat that the love of JESUS gave us out
of the excess of his mercy. (549–553)

The celebration of the Eucharist as the most precious object
proceeds through an enumeration of a series of classical and
theological exempla of symbolic narratives of eating. The Eucharist, in the rhetorical structure of Binet's text, is conceived and
presented as the culmination of founding and fundamental culinary narratives representing the interrelations between eating and
mourning, between eating and sacrifice, between eating and the
desire for immortality. The fact that the only objects considered
by Binet are culinary is symptomatic of the centrality of the act
of eating in Christian theology and eschatology and their Devout
articulation.

Once this most delicate and precious object is finally identified,
Binet moves on to establish the identity of the individual or
individuals who, in one way or another, have the most legitimate
claim to the right of ownership of this miraculous and magnificent
possession. And it is here that we encounter the strange and
alienating effects of the Devout logic taken to its ultimate expression: "Add to this the following sweet thought: it is that there
are several who have had the precious body of Jesus Christ in
their breast longer than Our Lady in the nine months of her
virginal pregnancy. For, by calculating, you will find that in nine
months there were only 275 days which make 6,600 hours,
[whereas for] someone who will have said the mass during forty
years, it makes . . ."[12]
    One is tempted to say that Binet represents the Devout "hon-
nêteté" recommended so strongly by Saint François de Sales in
its fullest manifestation. Taken to its limits, it constitutes itself by

a gesture of absolute exclusion; it determines its identity by its own identification, to be sure a phantasmagoric one, with a named and designated object which itself names and designates a mythical and founding moment of communal self-identification. The economy of desire in the Devout discourse gives way, in Binet's text, to a literalized economy of possession; it is replaced with a generalized economy of ownership founded on the privileges and rights of those who, in the ritualized sacramental context, displace and ultimately overshadow the immaculate conception and its mystery.

The Mystical Bees

The history of this Devout figuration of "honnêteté" goes beyond the mere evolution of manners and the decline of the theological strain at the end of the seventeenth century. Through a series of fascinating and revealing transmutations, it permeates the structure of the great debates of the reign of the Sun King from Pascal and Port-Royal to the Querelle du Pur Amour and the Querelle des Anciens et de Modernes. It is with Perrault, Fontenelle, and the triumphal assertions of the Moderns that food and eating irrevocably lose their theological density and give way to a relatively new or recaptured delectation of the "natural" taste of things.[13] This transformation of the figurative and cultural symbolism of food culminates in Marivaux's article from the *Mercure,* "Sur la Pensée Sublime" (On Sublime Thought).[14] In attempting to characterize the *sublime de l'homme* and to distinguish it from the *sublime de la nature,* Marivaux calls upon two privileged examples, theatrical representation and food:

> Imagine, madame, a banquet with thirty guests. Some of them will be able to distinguish finesses of the saucing in the dishes which will escape those whose less delicate palates will perceive only the

principal flavor. What is the result? The one of delicate palate is the more flattered without being any happier; each has his share of pleasure.

These two guests are the image of the spectators, from the man of gross to the man of fine feelings.

No cook can prepare a dish to everyone's taste. But his art, if he is good at it, is to succeed in having each of his dishes at least be acceptable to the general taste. His art is to assemble across the number of his dishes something for everyone.

By what we have just said, madame, you see that there can be no general and enthusiastic approval of sublime traits.[15]

The sublime, in Marivaux's text, is embodied by the chef's art and his skill at presentation and representation. Food and eating are no longer terms that simply designate or reflect the attitude of the one who eats, but instead they are marked by the one who prepares the food. This dialogic situation, completely absent in the Devout literature, marks the distance separating the Devout tradition of the early seventeenth century from the aesthetic debates of the late seventeenth and early eighteenth centuries. The relationships between table manners and sexual practices are replaced by those intimately binding taste in general and aesthetic taste in particular.

It is fitting to conclude this examination of the Devout tradition with a brief discussion of a short story in Saint François de Sales's *Traité de l'amour de Dieu,* a story that brings us back to the heart and its Christian and Devout mystical representations. The story, which appears in Book VII under the title, "Histoire merveilleuse du trépas d'un gentilhomme qui mourut d'amour sur le Mont d'Olivet" (Marvelous story of the death of a gentleman who died from love on the Mount of Olives),[16] is prefaced by a number of remarks that establish the specific importance of the narrative for the readers of the *Traité* and the exemplary value of its message. Furthermore, Saint François claims that the story, despite the fact that in his opinion it is admirable, is not very well known. In fact, he pretends that "even though the tale I am going to tell is neither as published nor as well attested as the greatness of the marvel that it contains would require" (698).[17] These introductory remarks are significant, for they construct and introduce the narrative frame required for a mystical appreciation and understanding of the story. The alleged poverty of commentary on the story serves to highlight the necessity of a return to the medieval hagiographic tradition with its emphasis on the miraculous. In other words, the rewriting of a well-established narrative, in the context of the *Traité de l'amour de Dieu,* signals the desire to reanimate and reactivate Devout belief and practice in terms of the exemplary powers of miracles and the miraculous. The story that Saint François is about to tell has to do with a transfer and displacement of the space of miracles and the modalities of such transfers and displacements.

The brief narrative tells the story of a knight who decides to visit the Holy land and to retrace the steps of Christ.[18] Before embarking on his journey, "he went to Confession and devoutly took communion" (698–699). He proceeds to visit the holy sites by following the chronological order of Christ's life from the annunciation to the crucifixion. Then he returns to the site of the Ascension, and "he began to pull into himself all the strength of his affections, as an archer pulls the string on his bow when he wants to launch his arrow; then standing, his eyes and hands stretched towards heaven: 'O Jesus,' he said, 'my sweet Jesus, I no longer know where to look for you and follow you on the earth; eh! Jesus, Jesus my love, grant this heart the wish to follow you and go after you on high.' And with these ardent words he so launched his heart to Heaven, like a sacred arrowhead, that like a divine archer, he hit close to his happy target" (700). He then collapses and dies. His friends, shocked by his sudden death, ask a physician to examine him and find the cause of his surprising

Christ as a child inhabiting man's heart.

collapse. Unable to find any physical explanation for the death, the physician asks his friends about his habits and customs. He then declares to them that "doubtless his heart burst from the excess and fervor of his love. And the better to attest his judgment he had him opened up, and found the brave heart open, with this sacred word engraved inside it: Jesus my love!" (701).[19]

The pilgrimage to the Holy Land thus becomes a mystical and devout exercise in the manner in which it reduces the spatial and geographical to the ahistorical and atemporal. Time and temporality are only the time of the life and death of Christ. The pilgrimage thus is a journey with an end and a closure, which are prescribed by the narrative of the life, death, and resurrection of Christ. The heart, the most privileged organ in the Devout mysticism of Saint François de Sales because it symbolizes Christ's passion and triumph, is now the locus of the allegorical mystical journey itself. The heart is the place and the surface of inscription of the quest for the lost and missing body of Christ, for the lost and missing mystical body. This quest, by its nostalgic desire for absolute closure and plenitude, leads directly to death, to the celebrated death of the mystic. The discursive and narrative allegorization of the journey to the center of Christianity, to the locus of the mystical experience itself, leads to the heart and its opening and inscription. The heart is no longer simply a symbol or a sign. It is now the stage where the battle is waged and where the mystic achieves the loss of the self and the ultimate withdrawal in the face of the divine. The mystic's heart is all he has to offer; it is all that is left after his sacrifice and disappearance. The mystic's heart is also the only thing he has left that can speak or, more precisely, that can inscribe and signify the triumph of the word. The language of the mystic's heart transforms and transfigures the body, or what is left of it, into words that sign the name of its rebirth.

ORIGO CASTI CORDIS.

Ego dormio et cor meum vigilat. Cant. 5.
Ego sto ad ostium et pulso, si quis aperue-
rit ianuam, intrabo ad illum. Apoc. 3.

Christ as a child sleeping on man's flaming heart.

From the Eaten Heart to the Revelation of the Heart

Saint François de Sales's rewriting of the medieval narratives locates the heart at the center of the mystical experience by making it the privileged space for the encounter with the divine.[20] Jean-Pierre Camus's heart, as we have seen, illustrates and valorizes the same practice by rejecting anthropophagy in favor of their mystical and Devout allegorizations. The heart, an organ at the center of life, is also the preferred organ for the most sophisticated death wish, the mystical quest par excellence. Yet a crucial difference separates the two texts and their authors. Camus's heart, in its intimate relations to the Eucharist and Christ's symbolic body, remains first and foremost an edible object, an object that is given to culinary transformations and modifications, an object that derives its symbolic powers from the central role that eating plays in Christian theology. Camus's heart is one that has to be eaten and interiorized within the body in order for it to reveal its real nature and presence, in order for it to become the effective presence of the divine body. Saint François de Sales's heart, on the other hand, is an object and an organ that must be opened up in order for it to reveal its secret and mystery. The miracle of the inscribed heart, of the heart that is no longer an organ of life and a symbol of vitality but rather the site of inscription and the signature of the divine—an inscription and a signature that can only come through death—consists in its separation from the body proper, its privileged status as that which survives through the letters on its surface, the letters that wound it and mark it eternally in the name of divine love. This heart, the heart of the letter and the word, the heart that is the vehicle for the name of the divine lover and the impact and deadly effects of divine love, is primarily an object that needs to be seen, an object that is in quest of a spectator and of a public, an object that has to be shown and revealed in its raw nudity and its savage but sweet presence. The Eucharist, in its full liturgical manifestation, is a spectacle without any human spectators. Everyone is a participant, and the only possible spectator is absent and missing; it is He in whose memory the sacrament is enacted and performed. The mystic's heart, in its double investment with visibility and death, rehearses the essential gesture of the performative aspect of the Eucharist by showing the ultimate effects of the interiorization of the mystical body of Christ and the drive toward visibility that such interiorization forces.

From the eaten heart to the visible and revealed heart, we have scanned the full power and diversity of the Christian appropriation of the heart and its symbolism. The two modalities of representation encapsulated in both narratives deploy the orientation and temporality of the inherited figurative powers of the heart as a means and a vehicle for the presentation of the mystical and Devout teleology.

FIVE

Trials and Tribulations of the Human Heart

When I see your Paris, continues this traveler, I think that I am
seeing a large animal; the streets are just so many veins in which
people circulate; how vivacious is the traffic in Paris! "You see,
I told him, this traffic occurs in the *heart* of Paris: there is an
even more effervescent one in the blood of the Parisians. They
are always agitated and always active; their actions follow upon
each other with so much speed that they begin a thousand
things before finishing one, and finish a thousand others before
they have even begun them."

DUFRESNY, *SERIOUS AND COMICAL AMUSEMENTS*

Theology and Teleology of the Heart

The theology of the sacred heart, invested and informed by the
foundational dimension of the Eucharist, plays, as we have seen
throughout, a determining role in the articulation and the specificity of the literary and cultural dimensions of the narratives of
the eaten heart from the Middle Ages to the early seventeenth
century. The Devout and mystical tradition, represented by Jean-
Pierre Camus and Saint François de Sales, defines and locates the

symbolic heart as the locus of exchange between the human and the divine, between the infinite and the finite, between the miracle of incarnation and transfiguration and the work and possibility of salvation. The mystical and Devout heart thus names the central organ of the mystical body of Christ, of the *ecclesia* and the Church, and as such it figures, in terms of the corporeal representations of the Incarnation, the full potential of Christological mediations. This figuration of the ultimate finality and closure of the Christian telos relies on a narrative strategy that derives its strength and vitality from the exploitation of the representation of Christ as the center and, as such, as the heart of human history.

This conception of Christ as both heart and center finds its most significant manifestation in the writings of Saint Bonaventure. In his commentaries devoted to the six days of Creation, Bonaventure argues for the logical, philosophical, and theological coherence of the figure of Christ as center and heart:

> The sun, in effect, is at the center of the planets and according to its movement, in an oblique circle, the generations are brought about. The physicist measures this generation. Of the planets, the one with the most powerful diffusion is the sun.
>
> In the same way, the diffusion of the heart is the most powerful, whatever the doctors may say. From it, in effect, the vital spirit is diffused through the arteries and the animal spirit through the nerves, although it is complemented in the brain; and from [the heart] also the natural spirit diffuses through the veins, though it is completed in the liver.
>
> Christ was the center at the moment of the incarnation . . . He is, like the heart, the center of the two vitalities.[1]

Heart and center are here one and the same thing. They both stand for the same function; they both ensure the coherence, hierarchy, and continuity of the flow and circulation necessary for life in its most generalized sense. As heart and center, Christ, through the Incarnation, ensures the survival and salvation of humanity in the same manner in which the heart controls the flow of the vital principle throughout the body. But what is perhaps most interesting and revealing in this passage is the medical context in which the figure of Christ as heart is deployed. The heart, in medical and physiological terms, is no longer the absolute center of the body. Its functions are supplemented and complemented by both the liver and the brain. It retains its centrality only in symbolic terms, only through the inherited powers of the figure of heart as absolute center. It also does so because it continues, according to Bonaventure, to function as the paradigm for circulation: the circulation of the vital principle, of the *pneuma;* the circulation of light; the circulation of symbolic and figurative structures of intelligibility underlying and informing incarnation and, consequently, the ultimate circulation and recuperation of bodies and the flesh. For indeed, as we have seen in the case of Augustine and his account of the integrity and totality of resurrection, restitution of the lost flesh, that is to say its circulation in a closed universe, and the economy of exchange between resurrected bodies and corpses, between living bodies and corpses, between eating and cannibalism, between violence and the closure of violence—all of these converge into a single moment defined by the Incarnation and its implications. Bonaventure's emphasis on the circulatory dimensions of the heart points to the full and filling capacity of the heart as a figurative organ at the center of the Christian figurative organism itself. But it also highlights one of its greatest weaknesses, its remarkable fragility. Thus the end of the reign of the heart as absolute center will come from the evidence of the medical and physiological sciences, the same sciences invoked by Bonaventure. Harvey's discovery of the circulation of the blood and the role of the heart as a mechanical pump, along with Descartes's physiology, will signal a major shift in the figurative and symbolic registers according to which the heart can be seen as the center of all vital activities. This shift will also mark the beginning of the rise of the brain as a symbolic rival and challenger to the absolute domination of the figure of the heart. One such moment is to be found in the biography of Descartes himself.

In his *Life of Monsieur Descartes,* Baillet tells of an interruption in the education of the philosopher—one that was brought about by grave political events, but which nevertheless remains, in the narrative of Descartes's life, an interruption:

> Mr. Descartes was in the first year of his philosophy courses when the news of the death of the king, killed Friday the 4th of May, 1610, brought to a halt the exercises of the *collège.* This good prince, when giving his house of La Flèche to the Jesuits, had expressed the desire that his heart, that of the queen and of his successors, be brought there after their deaths and kept in their church. The result was that the time that passed between the arrival of this sinister news and the transportation of the king's heart to La Flèche was spent in the *collège* in public prayers, in verse and prose funereal compositions, and in the preparations necessary to receive this deposit. The following Monday . . . classes were opened to take up the ordinary exercises of the *collège,* and Mr. Descartes continued the study of moral philosophy.[2]

Descartes's education was thus interrupted by the rituals and ceremonies of the burial of Henri IV at La Flèche. His study of "la philosophie morale" that ultimately would lead him to reject the heritage of philosophy and to try to inaugurate a new philosophy was marked by the circulation of the heart as paradigm of the vital principles of life as well as the privileged organ for the return to the absolute origin—the return, through the powers of the religious space, to the place where the political and the religious come together. The symbolic circulation of the heart, in this instance, constitutes a double interruption. First, it represents the end of a life, of a political life as an interruption that

*Saint Augustine, holding his flaming heart,
crushing the heretics.*

calls for a return to a chosen resting place invested with the powers to overcome death. Second, it marks the interruption of the flow and circulation of knowledge, an interruption that will become synonymous with Descartes's own founding philosophical gesture. And Descartes would finally, toward the end of his career, place the soul, the vital spirit and *pneuma* of the ancients, not in the heart but in the brain. The soul would come to rest, at least for a brief time thanks to Descartes, in the pineal gland itself, located by Descartes at the center or the heart of the brain. The logical and structural shifts of such a displacement are remarkable, and it is not my intention here to trace all of their implications. Instead I would like in this concluding chapter to point out some of the orientations that followed or at least accompanied the shift inaugurated by the emerging sciences of the seventeenth century. I will limit my observations to French thinkers, thus staying with Descartes's compatriots.

With the rise of the Moralist tradition in France and its acute concentration on the critical analysis of the passions, the heart undergoes some significant and informative transformations. While retaining its centrality as figure and guide to the character of the individual, it finds itself sharing center stage with a number of rivals and competitors. Reason and rationality emerge as one form of thought that is to be distinguished and separated from the heart and what it represents. Furthermore, the heart will come to occupy a new center defined by the Moralists' unremitting analysis of self-love and its social mechanisms. Thus, La Rochefoucauld, in the preface to the first edition of his *Maximes,* will describe his text as a portrait of the human heart: "Here is a portrait of the heart of Man that I give to the public under the name of Reflections or Moral Maxims . . . In a word, the best route for the reader to follow is to first keep in mind that not one of these maxims concerns him in particular, and that he is the only one excepted, although they appear to be general; after that, I reply to him that he will then be the first to subscribe to them and that he will believe that they are generous to the human heart."[3] The heart, in this instance, represents what La Rochefoucauld will include under the general term "moral," that is to say the modalities and mechanisms that define and characterize the social comportment of individuals as well as the motivations of the variety and diversity of social behavior. The heart now names the individual as a social and political entity. This orientation of the French Moralist literature is further developed by La Bruyère in his *Caractères,* particularly in the section entitled "Du Coeur" which is devoted in large part to an analysis of friendship. Whereas La Rochefoucauld generalizes the symbolic role of the heart, La Bruyère limits its intelligibility to the domain of friendship and thus restricts its economy of signification. La Bruyère, in this respect, continues to a certain extent the orientation opened up by Bacon in his essay *On Friendship.* What is most significant here is the almost complete absence of any theological or religious dimension in La Rochefoucauld's and La Bruyère's texts.[4] This theological dimension will resurface with Pascal, but with a new face and a new role.

For Pascal, the order of the heart is to be distinguished from the order of reason. To the heart belongs what he calls "instinct," that is, the certainty of the knowledge of some foundational principles such as space and time. Furthermore, the Pascalian order of the heart, in its specificity, accounts for a form of knowledge that is inaccessible to reason and rational analysis. The knowledge of the heart will ultimately provide, in its difference and independence from reason and rationality, firmly grounded belief:

> We know truth not only through reason but also by way of the heart. It is through this latter way that we know the first principles, and it is in vain that reason, which has no part of it, tries to combat

them.

For the knowledge of the first principles, such as that there is a space, time, movement, number, [is] as solid as any that our reasoning provides us. And it is on this knowledge of the heart and of instinct that reason has to rely and found all of its discourse.

This impotence should only serve then to humiliate reason, which wishes to judge all, but not to combat our certainty, as if there were no other faculty than reason capable of instructing us. Would that it had pleased God that we have no need of it and that we knew all things through instinct and sentiment. But nature refused us this good; it gave us on the contrary very few forms of knowledge of this sort. All the others can only be acquired by way of reason.

And that is the reason for which those to whom God gave religion by the way of the sentiment of the heart are in fact most content and rightfully persuaded. But to those who do not have it, we can only offer it by way of reason, awaiting the time when God may give it to them through the feelings of the heart. Without which faith would be only human and useless for the purpose of salvation.[5]

The order of the heart constitutes for Pascal the foundation of what we might call the anthropology of belief. The uncertainty of human knowledge derived from reason and rational demonstration is opposed to the immediacy of the knowledge of the heart, to the knowledge of instinct. Furthermore, and beyond the dialectical opposition between the two orders, between reason and the heart and the manner in which the heart and its knowledge show the limits of rational knowledge, the order of the heart remains the privileged domain where the divine and the human meet and cooperate. The order and the knowledge of the heart come from God and therefore do not require the intervention of reason. The order and the knowledge of the heart are superior to reason precisely because of their religious and theological finality, precisely because they signal the encounter and the triumph of belief over and against reason. Those blessed with the knowledge of the heart are, as Pascal says, "bien heureux et bien légitimement persuadés" ("very happy and quite legitimately persuaded") (351). They do not need nor do they desire to be persuaded by reason or rhetoric. They are firm in their knowledge because their knowledge is their belief.

Pascal's separation of reason and the heart and the priority he grants the order of the heart are symptomatic of the displacements and shifts in the figurative status of the heart. The heart is no longer the organ at the center of an organism. With Pascal, it becomes the ground and the name for a form of knowledge that defies and escapes reason. It becomes the form of knowledge that is at the limits of all knowledge, since its undeniable existence serves to humiliate the arrogance of reason in order to reestablish the hierarchy informed by the centrality of belief. The Pascalian order of the heart, while recuperating some of the symbolic functions of the heart, introduces a new economy of figuration and representation in terms of which what cannot be rationally represented simply because it is felt and thought otherwise firmly grounds the most important knowledge. The Pascalian order of the heart, at the crossroads of the scientific and the mystical writings of Pascal, opens up the way for a philosophical and anthropological discourse that will take as its object not normative knowledge but instead the insights and the forms of belief that precede it. Pascal's order of the heart, in this perspective, names both the end of an era and the beginning of a new order. It remains significant and relevant because it does not limit its motivation or insight to the mere confirmation of the necessity of belief. Instead, it adopts the existence of belief as a dynamic point of departure for the investigation of knowledge itself. It is as if, instead of being the agent for mourning a loss, the Pascalian order of the heart mourns the false belief in the limitless powers of rationality and celebrates the infinite powers of belief and insight that still inhabit and only come with and through the heart.

Incarnation, Sacred Heart, and the Eucharist

With Pascal and the French Moralists, the heart becomes the locus of a double knowledge. The order of the heart thus opens up unto a form of knowledge and cognition that humbles and goes beyond reason. But the heart remains nevertheless the seat of all passions and thus continues to function, at least in the conceptual framework informing the writings of the French Moralists, as the privileged motor of all forms of human comportment. The observation of the heart and its movements suffices to explain and account for the way of being, of the interplay between being and appearance, central to the analysis of the Moralists. The heart, in this context, at the same time replaces and emblematizes the secret motivations of human behavior, its vicissitudes and finality. The heart of the Moralists, because it reveals what is hidden beneath what shows itself, and because it seeks to reveal itself, is constituted as the nucleus, as the space of individual interiority that guides and manipulates the exhibition of both speech and body in the social order.

This "heart" of the Moralists, as a result of its purely ethical and figurative conception, stands in direct opposition to the Cartesian description of the heart as a mere organ of the body. Descartes, in his treatise on the *Passions of the Soul*, by locating the *pneuma* of the Ancients, or the soul, in the pineal gland at the center of the brain, in effect rejects all the received representations of the human heart and its assumed relations to the passions. For Descartes, the heart is simply a motor, a mechanical pump that controls the circulation of the blood and manages its distribution in the human body. From the point of view of

Cartesian physiology, the heart of the Moralists is but a fiction, a pure figure investing the physiological organ with powers that are neither observable nor demonstrable. In this context, the heritage of Descartes and his physiology will culminate in a philosophy and an ethics founded on the central role of the brain in the analysis of human comportment. Thus, the discovery of the circulation of the blood by Harvey and Descartes's tortured descriptive analysis in his treatise on the *Passions* inaugurate the rivalry and rupture between the heart and the brain, between the two centers competing for the privilege of explaining human behavior. Between the Moralists on the one hand, and Descartes and his heritage on the other, we witness the reconfiguration or even the redefinition of the status of the human heart at the beginning of the modern period in Western thought. The duel between the two schools constitutes not only our heritage but also our ongoing effort to understand and represent the ways in which we interact with one another in society.

I shall return one last time, after this brief historical interlude, to the depiction of the heart in the Devout and spiritual tradition as illustrated by the texts of François de Sales and Jean-Pierre Camus. For despite their apparent similarities, these two texts put forward two distinct models of the heart, two models whose function is to describe and exemplify the spiritual movement par excellence, that is, the negation of self and the encounter with the divine presence within the body of the believer. The annihilation of the self, the precondition of the mystical exercise as well as the ultimate goal of the spiritual quest, finds in Jean-Pierre Camus and François de Sales significantly different, if not opposed, manifestations. For Camus, as we have seen, the order that dominates the spiritual journey is secret; it is grounded in an ultimate radical gesture of withdrawal and retreat from the social world. The subject is always alive, but it now hosts the heart of the divine lover. The eaten heart, in short, is none other than the Sacred Heart. It is in effect the heart of the Sacred itself, its ultimate manifestation in the body of the believer. Thus, in Camus's text, the fundamental and founding role of the Eucharist emerges as unavoidable. The whole narrative, with all of its erudite details and allusions, is there in order to point to and to name the most secret and the most desired object, the missing mystical body of Christ.

In François de Sales's case, the principal subject of the exemplary narrative is no longer alive; he cannot survive the spiritual journey of his pilgrimage because he consciously elects to sacrifice himself. And it is thanks to his death, thanks to death itself, that he succeeds in publicizing the radical impact of the ultimate union with the divine body, a union that signals death and that is made manifest through the trace and the signature of the divine visitation inscribed for all to see on the surface of the believer's heart. François de Sales's pilgrimage finds its happy end in the effects of the excess of divine love. The pilgrim dies because his heart shatters, because his body, in its natural state, can no longer accommodate or support the presence of the desired divine. He also dies because, in his death, he manifests Christ's divine powers. Loss of self is here to be taken literally.

In Camus's *Spectacles d'horreurs*, the split between being and appearance, and the accompanying ambivalences and ambiguities of the interaction between the social and spiritual orders, are ultimately preserved and maintained as such. These differences are reinforced in large measure by the desire for reconciliation animating the narrative, whereas, in de Sales's writings, the social order is there simply to witness the power and the reality of spiritual life. The transformed heart, the heart that writes its love in a violent and final burst (literally), is first and foremost a visible object. It intends its visibility and constitutes its revelation as a spectacle. From one heart to the other, from the beating heart of the body to the heart signed by and with Christ's love, there

Marie of the Incarnation holding her flaming heart.

is only one step to be taken. This leap toward and into the overwhelming presence of the divine lover is, in the logic of François de Sales's text and the theology underlying it, a form of surrender to pure visibility, a letting go of one's self and one's life in favor of the desire to make visible to all the otherwise inaccessible space of pure interiority.

Camus's "eaten heart" was and remains an edible object. It enters the body through the mouth, the organ of speech and the site of original sin. This Eucharistic dimension of the "eaten heart" bypasses and excludes any form of visibility. For the Eucharist interiorizes a mystical body within the human one: it incorporates the human and divine bodies into one. But this incorporation, realized through the magical powers of speech and its effects, remains a mystery. And a mystery never fully reveals itself. Bacon, as we saw in his essay on friendship, was already alarmed by the perverse and harmful effects of words that inhabit the heart and thus circulate within the body without ever finding an appropriate outlet or channel through which they can be seen or recognized by an other. This is perhaps why the heart that is dominated by the Eucharistic logic is destined for retreat and secrecy, as in the image of Crisele in Camus's tragic tale of love and jealousy. This heart exists in order to host and hide an other. It survives because it must live for the sake of that other. In this context, Crisele's quest represents a spiritual adventure in search of the missing body of Christ, an adventure dedicated to the repetition of this quest and the celebration of the loss that only the Eucharist can make up for.

Dante, in his *Vita Nuova,* founded his quest on the determining moment of exteriorizing his desire and love for Beatrice. A spectator detached from his heart and witness to the violent spectacle of his phantasm, he fully realized the necessity of "transparence" that animated his marvelous vision. In the same manner, François de Sales's narrative projects the image and its effects, the image of death as well as the image of the writing of this unique and most desirable death. Between the two, and in the new space of visibility, emerges a possibility for narration and writing, a place for the reception of the letters and words capable of telling a life and its history. This space within the opened body and of the opened heart will become, in the development of the theology and imagery of the Christian cult inspired by the writings of de Sales and others like him, the privileged locus of narrative and figural exploitations of the Sacred Heart. The heart will be transformed into a page upon which the believer will be able to read the endless variations of the exemplary story of the life of Christ. But this heart that is also and especially an image will come to represent, in the popular culture as well as in the spiritual and Devout tradition, the space of reciprocity between divine reflection and the human gaze. The heart, receptacle of the image and the figure of the death of the body, ultimately reveals the desire for visibility animating the divine, in its Christian conception, and the effects of such a desire. François de Sales's tale celebrates the signed and shattered heart as the ultimate form of the loss of self and as the most appropriate figure for all the mystical expressions designating the abolition of the self in favor of the divine.

This shattered and inscribed heart opens up a space for the visibility of the divine and of its writing in images and words, in combinations of images and words located within the heart. The eaten heart, on the contrary, hides and covers up its mysterious interiorization. Between the two hearts, between pure visibility and the image on the one hand, and the secret and its complementary withdrawal from the world on the other, are drawn the lines separating the transparency through the image and the absolute mystery of interiorization of the missing divine body. Between the two hearts and the models they make possible, a whole intellectual history is waiting to be read.

Notes

Introduction

1. Plutarch, *Moralia* XIII, "The Eating of the Flesh I" (Cambridge, Mass.: Harvard University Press/Loeb Classical Library, 1969), pp. 559–561.
2. Aristotle, *De Motu Animalium,* trans. Martha Nussbaum (Princeton, N.J.: Princeton University Press, 1978), pp. 50–52. Aristotle proceeds in the following section of *De Motu* to identify the heart as the source and origin of sperm, the principal source of life: "In the case of the heart, the reason for this is clear: in it are the origins of the senses. And there is evidence that the generative part, too, is of this kind: for the force of semen comes forth from it like a living creature" (p. 54). For a general survey of the role of the heart in Greek medical literature, see C. R. S. Harris, *The Heart and the Vascular System in Ancient Greek Medicine* (Oxford: Oxford University Press, 1973). See also David F. Furley's introduction to *Galen's On Respiration and the Arteries* (Princeton, N.J.: Princeton University Press, 1984) for a discussion of Aristotle's sometimes ambiguous identification of the soul and the heart and its history and influence in biological and medical literature from Galen to Harvey, pp. 20ff.
3. I do not mean to imply here that the only function of the funerary meal is the celebration of survival. It is evident that the funerary

meal is also a basic memory tool that allows the community to recall its ancestry, to relive the memories of its past and to maintain a continuity between that past and the present. In a number of "primitive" societies, for example, it is common to eat the ashes of the dead with food. In classical antiquity, the cult of the dead called for a strict separation between the living and the dead: "We should greatly deceive ourselves if we thought that these funeral repasts were nothing more than a sort of commemoration. The food that the family brought was really for the dead—exclusively for him. What proves this is, that the milk and wine were poured out upon the earth of the tomb; that the earth was hollowed out so that the solid food might reach the dead; that if they sacrificed a victim, all its flesh was burnt, so that none of the living could have any part of it; that they pronounced certain consecrated formulas to invite the dead to eat and drink; that if the entire family were present at the meal, no one touched the food . . . The Roman tomb also had its *culina,* a species of kitchen, of a particular kind, and entirely for the use of the dead." Fustel de Coulanges, *The Ancient City* (Baltimore: Johns Hopkins University Press, 1980 [1864]), pp. 11–12.

4. For the theoretical elaboration of the dynamic interplay between introjection and incorporation, see Nicolas Abraham and Maria Torok, *L'écorce et le noyau* (Paris: Aubier-Flammarion, 1978).

5. For an English translation of the tale, see Miriam Lichtheim, *Ancient Egyptian Literature* (Berkeley: University of California Press, 1976), II, 202–211. All quotations in the text are from this translation. For discussions of the tale, its mythological dimensions as well as its relation to the story of Joseph in Genesis, see, among others, William Kelly Simpson, ed., *The Literature of Ancient Egypt: An Anthology of Stories, Instructions, and Poetry* (New Haven: Yale University Press, 1972); Gustave Lefebvre, *Romans et contes égyptiens de l'époque pharaonique* (Paris: Maspero, 1949), "Le conte des deux frères," pp. 137–158; G. Maspero, *Les contes populaires de l'égypte ancienne* (Paris: Maisonneneuve et Larose, 1911); A. M. Blackman, *The Literature of the Ancient Egyptians* (New York: Arno Books, 1977); A. Erman, *Die Literatur der Aegypter* (Leipzig: J. C. Hinrichs, 1923); G. Paris, "Le conte du trésor du roi Rhampsinite," *Revue d'Histoire des Religions* 55 (1907).

6. On the function and symbolic role of the heart in ancient Egypt see Alexandre Piankoff, *Le Coeur dans les textes égyptiens depuis l'Ancien Empire jusqu'à la fin du Nouvel Empire* (Paris: Presses Universitaires de France, 1930): "It appears from the preceding examples that for the Egyptians the heart had a triple role—it was first the central organ of man, second, the vital center, the seat of all emotions, and finally, the seat of intelligence. The same ideas concerning the heart are found among primitive peoples, among the peoples of antiquity, and in folklore. Thus for the Babylonians, who in their civilization are the closest to the Egyptians, the heart played a very important role; they considered it, along with the liver, to be the soul or the principle of life. For the Hebrews, the heart was the symbol of life. This is clearly expressed in Proverbs 4:23: 'Guard your heart more than any other thing, For from it spring the sources of life'" (p. 52). And "thus, in the texts from the Pyramids, the oldest known in Egypt, we can distinguish three different cases relating to the heart: the dead person, in the first place, receives his heart purified and divinized and, through this act, comes back to life. Second, he fears that his heart might be stolen by adversaries in the other world, and finally, he eats the hearts of his adversaries" (p. 63); my translations. See also Michel Malaise, *Les scarabées de coeur dans l'Egypte ancienne* (Brussels: Fondation égyptologique Reine Elisabeth, 1978), especially pp. 14 and 41; J. Doresse, "Le coeur et les anciens égyptiens," in a special issue of *Etudes Carmélitaines* (1950) devoted to the heart.

1. The Lure of the Heart

1. In Genesis (3:1–7), the temptation of eating the apple is explicitly described in terms of the eyes and their symbolic powers: "Then the serpent said to the woman, 'No! You will not die! God knows in fact that on the day you eat it your eyes will be opened and you will be like gods, knowing good and evil.'" What follows describes the discovery of the body and its nudity: "The woman saw that the tree was good to eat and pleasing to the eye, and that it was desirable for the knowledge that it could give. So she took some of its fruit and ate it. She gave some also to her husband who was with her,

and he ate it. Then the eyes of both of them were opened and they realized that they were naked."

2. For a detailed discussion of the interplay and relations between sexuality and mortality in the biblical narrative, see Howard N. Wallace's *The Eden Narrative*, Harvard Semitic Monographs (Atlanta: Scholars' Press, 1985), especially pp. 143–172. Wallace provides a succinct overview of the various interpretations of the text in the process of developing his own reading. Concerning the nakedness of Adam and Eve, he hints at the possibility of a prior sexual act: "The sin itself does not directly involve the naked state of the couple. This situation is employed in part as an explanation of the origin of clothing. In addition a touch of irony is evident. Instead of knowing good and evil like the gods (3:5), they know only human shame and fear. However, neither of these last points in itself, nor even both together, is sufficient to give rise to the prominence of the motif of nakedness in the story. More likely they have arisen in an effort to overcome a feature of the narrative employed in other renditions which presented some difficulty for the J writer or those upon whom he was dependent. There could even have been a sexual element in the nakedness that is hidden now by the aetiology and irony" (p. 145).

3. The Eucharist retains redemptive powers because the original sin, the eating of the apple, was not absolute. As Augustine puts it in the *City of God* (New York: Penguin Books, 1984): "Yet man did not fall away to the extent of losing all being; but when he had turned towards himself his being was less real than when he adhered to him who exists in a supreme degree. And so, to abandon God and to exist in oneself, that is to please oneself, is not immediately to lose all being; but it is to come nearer to nothingness" (XIV, 13, p. 572). In Augustine's terms, eating the apple signifies a turn toward the self, a turn in the direction of nothingness in the sense that eating the apple implies the loss of the view of God. The Eucharist will come to represent the countermeasure to this fall, the return to the original through a surrender into the mystery of incorporation that would lead to the reunion with God.

4. The duality of Christ, as is well known, gave rise to endless polemics. It also played a crucial role in making possible the transfer of

Notes to Pages 21–23

theological categories into the political domain, precisely because, in the logic of Christian narrative, it is meant to function as a substitution and a recovery. On this question see Ernst Kantorowicz, *The King's Two Bodies: A Study in Medieval Political Theology* (Princeton, N.J.: Princeton University Press, 1957), especially pp. 42–61.

5. All references to the text are to Renaut de Beaujeu, *Le Lai d'Ignaure ou lai du prisonnier,* ed. Rita Lejeune (Brussels: Palais des Académies, 1938). Quotations are my translations from this edition, with line numbers given in parentheses following the quote.

6. The Dionysian mirror has been extensively studied and compared to the other mirrors of antiquity, namely the mirrors of Narcissus and Medusa. On this question in general and on the relations between the three mirrors and the manner in which they lend themselves to a number of mythological and philosophical interpretations concerning the conception and articulation of subjectivity, see, among others, J. Pépin, "Plotin et le miroir de Dionysos," *Revue Internationale de Philosophie* 22 (1970); P. Hadot, "Le mythe de Narcisse et son interprétation par Plotin," *Nouvelle Revue de Psychanalyse* 13 (1976); and J.-P. Vernant, *L'individu, la mort, l'amour en grèce ancienne* (Paris: Gallimard, 1989), especially pp. 168ff. For a general survey devoted to Greek mirrors and their various uses and valorizations, see A. Delatte, *La Catopromancie et ses dérives* (Paris: E. Droz, 1932).

For a taste of the neoplatonic interpretation of Dionysus' sacrifice by the Titans, consider this passage from Proclus' *Commentary on Plato's Parmenides,* trans. G. R. Morrow and J. M. Dillon (Princeton, N.J.: Princeton University Press, 1987): "For, to put it briefly, Soul is third in rank from the One and is naturally actualized in this way: For the One is one only and precedes thought, Intellect thinks all ideas as one, and Soul sees them all one by one. So division is the peculiar function of Soul, since she lacks the power of thinking all things simultaneously in unity and has been allotted the thinking of them separately—all, because she imitates Intellect, and separately, for this is her peculiar property; for the power to divine and define appears first in Soul. This is why the theologians say that at the dismemberment of Dionysus his intellect [heart] was preserved undivided through the foresight of Athena and that his soul was the first to be divided, and certainly the division into seven is proper primarily to Soul" (III, 808–809, p. 174). Proclus' interpretation is significant because it highlights the calculus involved and implied in the evaluation of Dionysus' sacrifice. Instead of division, we encounter subtraction in Plotinus and also in Pseudo-Dionysus. In Plotinus' *On Beauty* (Cambridge, Mass.: Harvard University Press/Loeb Classical Library, 1966), Narcissus' and Dionysus' mirrors are elliptically invoked in order to valorize a form of Platonic subtraction: "So you too must cut away any excess and straighten the crooked and clear the dark and make it bright, and never stop 'working on your own statue'" (p. 259). Plotinus' metaphors prepare the way for the mystical appropriation of this passage in the *Pseudo-Dionysian Mystical Theology*, 1025B. The Plotinian and especially mystical interpretation of the statue in Dionysian terms define sculpture and subtraction as the model and paradigm for meditation and contemplation, that is to say the mystical cognition of subjectivity in relation to the divine.

7. For a comprehensive study of the Titans' sacrifice of the child Dionysus and its place in Greek mythology and philosophy, see Marcel Detienne's *Dionysos mis à mort* (Paris: Gallimard, 1987); translated as *Dionysus Slain* (Baltimore: Johns Hopkins University Press, 1989). See also Walter Burkert, *Homo Necans: The Anthropology of Ancient Greek Sacrificial Ritual and Myth,* trans. Peter Bing (Berkeley: University of California Press, 1983 [1972]). Burkert comments on the singularity of the Dionysian sacrifice in the following terms: "The Classical Greeks had virtually insurmountable inhibitions: ever since Homer, gods had been immortal by definition. How, then, could a god die or become the victim of a cannibalistic meal? Such myths become themselves 'unspeakable,' *arrhetos*. But there was a single god of whom this story was told: Dionysus. The Titans lured the child Dionysus away from his throne, tore him apart, and ate him. As we can gather from allusions, this myth, apparently handed down in the Orphic mysteries, was known in the fifth century, even if it was officially ignored" (p. 225).

8. Quoted in Detienne, *Dionysus Slain*, pp. 86–87.

9. These identifications extend to a number of Orphic and Pythago-

rean taboos, most notably eggs and beans: "But my companions at one of Sossius Senecio's dinners suspected me of being committed to the beliefs of the Orphics and Pythagoreans and holding the egg taboo, as some hold the heart and brain, because I thought it to be the first principle of creation. And Alexander the Epicurean teasingly recited: 'Now eating the beans is much like eating parent's heads. For these people call eggs 'beans' *(kuamoi)* punning on the word 'conception' *(kuesis),* and they think that eating eggs in no way differs from using the creatures which produce the eggs.'" Plutarch, *Moralia* VIII (Cambridge, Mass.: Harvard University Press/Loeb Classical Library, 1969), II: 3, 635.

10. On incorporation, see Nicolas Abraham and Maria Torok, *L'écorce et le noyau* (Paris: Aubier Flammarion, 1978).

11. This initial mourning takes the form of fasting, of abstinence: "'I do not know whether he is dead or alive! / And each one of us received from him all she could desire; / Now help me to carry out my mourning; / Because each of us got joy out of him / [Therefore] let our pain be shared.' / They swore to the messenger / That they would never eat again / Until the moment when they would be able to know / Whether he was dead or alive, or to see [him]. / And then they began to fast" (522–531).

12. The closure of the narrative is named directly in the poem: "And the other wept for his [Ignaure's] loving heart: / There would never exist again one of such value. / 'Alas! We have changed you so much; / Their vengeance was too cruel. The jealous [husbands]! But we will not eat: / And thus will we avenge ourselves'" (597–602).

13. Rita Lejeune, the editor of the *Lai d'Ignaure,* considers some of these features either "pleasant" or simply in bad taste: "The confession scene, Ignaure's replies to his furious lovers, these certainly constitute a theme foreign to the legend of the eaten heart . . ., a theme that Renaut elaborated considerably because it pleased him. This is why, contrary to what is normally said, it isn't certain that the story of the "Dismembering of Ignaure," which only shows up in the *Lai*—let us insist on this one more time—is also a primitive characteristic. It seems to me to be above all an instance of bad taste on Renaut's part" (*Lai d'Ignaure,* pp. 35–36). More recently,

Charles Muscatine has written: "The *Lai d'Ignaure* is a strange, part courtly, part brutal, priapic version of the 'eaten heart' motif of romance," in *The Old French Fabliaux* (New Haven: Yale University Press, 1986), pp. 13–14.

14. It goes without saying that Dionysus' heart played a crucial role in the formation of the cult of the sacred heart. For the twelfth century, one can also think of the first stories concerning the *extractio cordis* as a target of a poem like the *Lai d'Ignaure:* "In Dorothée de Montau, the issue is at once that of stigmatization and of the exchange of hearts between God and his servant. Several witnesses claim to have seen bleeding wounds under her tunic, reflections of the wounds of love that God had inflicted upon her. As for the *extractio cordis,* it is mentioned both by very simple folk and by the theologians of her entourage, who insist on the physiological reality of the phenomenon. This latter was, moreover, the object of a specific article (article 21), concerning which most of those who had known the recluse of Marienwerder when she was alive were interrogated" (André Vauchez, *La sainteté en Occident aux derniers siècles du moyen âge* [Paris: Boccard/Ecole Française de Rome, 1981], p. 517; my translation). We remember that after eating the heart of their dead lover, the women "regain" their heart ("Quant lor cuer furent revenu" [560]).

15. We shall follow, in the next two chapters, the literary and theological developments of the legend of the eaten heart in which the *Lai d'Ignaure* comes first in a sequence of texts that display a series of displacements, inversions, and perversions and that culminate with Jean-Pierre Camus's "Le coeur mangé" (1630) in *Les Spectacles d'Horreur* (Geneva: Slatkine Reprints, 1973). My argument is that the double origin of the legend, Christian and Dionysian, accounts for the interplay between figuration and disfiguration that is constant in all versions of the legend. Furthermore, between the *Lai* and Camus's text, we have the two extremes as well as the two texts that mirror each other the most precisely because they rehearse the founding and closure of the sequence.

16. All references to the *Roman* are to the partial modern French translation in "Le Coeur mangé," pp. 241–253; the English translations given in the text are mine.

2. *"Vide Cor Tuum"*

1. For a detailed discussion of the relations between *saber* and *sabor* see Pierre Guiraud, *Sémiologie de la sexualité* (Paris: Payot, 1978), especially pp. 141–164.
2. *Le Coeur mangé,* p. 248.
3. *The Decameron,* trans. John Payne, rev. and ed. Charles Singelton (Berkeley: University of California Press, 1982). Page references in the text are to this edition.
4. *Dante's Vita Nuova,* trans. M. Musa (Bloomington: Indiana University Press, 1973); page references in the text are to this edition. Dante's vision has given rise to extensive debates. For a sampling, see, among many others, G. C. Spivak, "Finding Feminist Readings: Dante-Yeats," *Social Text* 2 (1980); B. Nolan, "The *Vita Nuova:* Dante's Book of Revelation," *Dante Studies* 88 (1970); R. P. Harrison, *The Body of Beatrice* (Baltimore: Johns Hopkins University Press, 1988). For a discussion of *Ego dominus tuus* and *Vide cor tuum,* see T. Hyde, *The Poetic Theology of Love* (Newark, N.J.: Rutgers University Press, 1986), pp. 45–72.
5. Francis Bacon, *The Essays,* ed. with an introduction by John Pitcher (New York: Penguin, 1985), p. 141. Subsequent quotations in the text will give page references from this edition. Pitcher comments in the following terms on Bacon's Pythagorean quote: "Deep within the body, there are some meanings so obscure and so frightening that they cannot be tamed at all. In *Of Friendship,* probably the greatest of the *Essays,* Bacon comes very close to saying that words lacerate the body, wound it, eat it within when it refuses to disclose meaning" (p. 41).
6. Montaigne, *Essais* (Paris: Presses Universitaires de France, 1965), "De l'Amitié," I: XXVIII, 275; my translation.
7. Augustine, *The City of God* (New York: Penguin Books, 1984), XXII, 20. Jean Pépin, in his *Théologie cosmique et théologie chrétienne* (Paris: Presses Universitaires de France, 1964), notes the monetary metaphor in Augustine's text and compares it to Porphyry: "Augustine, as we know, deals with the difficulty by comparing the two men to a creditor and a debtor, and flesh to a sum of money lent by the one to the other; but Porphyry suggested this judicial

solution in the very terms of his exposé, where he deals with
reclamation, restition, etc." (p. 451; my translation).

8. For a discussion of the relations between belief, *fides,* and money,
see Emile Benveniste's essay entitled "Créance et Croyance" in his
Vocabulaire des institutions Indo-Européennes (Paris: Minuit, 1969).
For a discussion of money, economy, usury, and medieval theology,
see Jacques Le Goff's *Pour un autre Moyen âge: Temps, travail et
culture en Occident* (Paris: Gallimard, 1977), especially pp. 46–65
and 91–107. See also his more recent study, *La Bourse et la vie*
(Paris: Hachette, 1986).

3. *A Lover's Course: "Le Coeur mangé"*

1. Camus has been largely ignored by modern criticism. Most critics,
with the exception of a select few, consider him unoriginal and
secondary. Thus, for example, Antoine Adam's assessment: "Camus
wrote with a marvelous and deplorable facility . . . He hardly
needed a single night to write a novella, and fifteen days to compose
a volume of eight hundred to a thousand pages," *Histoire de la
littérature française au XVIIème siècle,* vol. 1 (Paris: Editions Mondiales, 1962), p. 421. Only René Godenne, in his *Histoire de la
Nouvelle Française aux XVII et XVIII siècles* (Geneva: Droz, 1970),
gives serious attention to Camus's fictional works. Philippe Ariès,
in his *The Hour of Our Death,* trans. Helen Weaver (New York:
Vintage Books, 1982 [1977]), discusses some of Camus's tales, but
his knowledge of Camus's texts seems to be surprisingly limited.
For a general survey on Camus, see Jean Descrains's edition of his
Homélies des Etats Généraux (Paris: Droz, 1970). See also Sylvie
Robic's thesis "Le salut par l'excès: Analyse d'une poétique de la
dévotion dans l'oeuvre de Jean-Pierre Camus," presented at the
Ecole des Hautes Etudes en Sciences Sociales, Paris, in 1994. On
Camus's life, the best statement remains that of Perrault in his *Les
Hommes illustres* (Paris: Antoine Dezallier, 1696). Since Camus is
unknown to most readers, I will quote generously from Perrault's
text: "At this time, novels became very fashionable, beginning with
Astrée, whose beauty was the delight and craze of France and even
of the furthest foreign countries. The bishop of Belley, considering

this reading material to be an obstacle to the progression of the love of God in people's souls, but yet considering it impossible to deter young people from an amusement so pleasant and in accordance witih the inclinations of their age group, sought the means to divert them by writing stories with love in them, which thus would be read, but which would insensibly raise the heart to God through pious sentiment adroitly inserted, and by the Christian catastrophes of all of their adventures. For it always happened that one or the other of the lovers, or both together, having considered the nothingness of the things of this world, the malice of men, the peril that one always runs of losing salvation by walking in the ways of the century, resolved to give themselves wholly to God, renouncing everything and embracing the religious life. This was a lucky artifice that his ardent charity, which devoted him entirely to everyone, had him invent and put successfully to work. For his books passed into everyone's hands, and as they were full not only of highly pleasant incidents, but also of good maxims very useful for directing one's life, they bore considerable fruit, and were a kind of counterpoison to the reading of novels" (pp. 9–10; my translation).

Here are some of Camus's juicy titles: *L'Amphithéâtre sanglant* (1630), *Le Bouquet d'histoires agréables* (1662), *Les Leçons exemplaires* (1632), *Les Occurences remarquables* (1628), *Les Rencontres funestes* (1644), *La Tour des miroirs* (1631), *Le Verger historique* (1644).

2. Camus presents his narratives as lessons or representative examples. In his preface to another collection of tales entitled *Récits historiques*, published in 1644, he defines narrative in the following terms: "The relation of an action, stripped of all artifice, and even of the concerns of eloquence, is commonly called a narrative, and this is the name that I thought it appropriate to give to these stories of which I here am making a collection"; quoted in G. Hainsworth's *Les "Novelas Exemplares" de Cervantes en France au XVIIe siècle* (Paris: Champion, 1933), p. 150.

3. René Favert in his introduction to a selection of Camus's short stories, *Trente Nouvelles de Jean-Pierre Camus* (Paris: Vrin, 1977), p. 8.

4. All subsequent references to Camus's text will be to *Les Spectacles*

d'Horreur. Avec une introduction de René Godenne (Geneva: Slatkine Reprints, 1973); note that the preface is unpaginated. English translations are mine.

5. In his preface to the volume, Camus compares his narrative method to that of a surgeon: "Good surgeons heal by manipulating the wounds of the injured, and by extracting the blood from the veins of the sick. We will imitate them by taking good examples from the most horrible actions furnished by the great theater of the world" (Preface). The medical metaphor is significant here because, as we shall see, the "theater of the world" will turn out to be Boccaccio's *Decameron* and the courtly tradition.

6. Philippe Ariès has noted, albeit in a different context, the change in the status of death in Camus's writings: "Death is no longer a special event. As we have seen, only three out of all the deaths in Camus were from natural causes. Nor is death any longer a moment of moral and psychological concentration, as it was in the *artes moriendi*. Death has become inseparable from violence and pain . . . These violent scenes excited spectators and aroused primitive forces whose sexual nature seems obvious today" (*The Hour Of Our Death*, p. 372). It seems that Ariès neglects or ignores the devout theology and spirituality motivating Camus's writings.

7. Camus pretends that his story is true: "Memnon, young gentleman from a province beyond the Loire, that I do not wish to name" (p. 28). This is a conventional strategy in the tradition of the sixteenth-century novella. According to R. Dubuis: "It is traditional and seemly, in all medieval literature, from the chanson de geste on, to affirm loudly that the story being told is perfectly authentic. *Les Cent nouvelles nouvelles* are no exception to the rule"; "Réalité et Réalisme dans *les Cent nouvelles nouvelles*," in *La Nouvelle française à la Renaissance*, études réunies par Lionello Sozzi (Geneva: Slatkine, 1981), p. 95. Despite Camus's rhetoric, it is evident that his story is a reworking of a number of older texts. On the legend of the eaten heart in French medieval literature, see John E. Matzke's "The Legend of the Eaten Heart," *Modern Language Notes*, 26:1 (1911), 1–8. In addition to Boccaccio's text and the *Roman du châtelain de Couci et de la dame de Fayel*, Matzke identifies some oriental equivalents to the legend.

8. Agrippa d'Aubigné, *Les Tragiques* (Paris: Garnier Flammarion, 1968). The quote comes from the first book, *Misères,* pp. 520–546; my translation. For a general discussion of the religious wars and the use of metaphors of cannibalism and anthropophagy, see Frank Lestringant's "Catholiques et Cannibales: Le thème du cannibalisme dans le discours protestant au temps des Guerres de religion," in *Pratiques et discours alimentaires* à *la Renaissance* (Paris: Maisonneuve et Larose, 1982), pp. 233–246. For a fascinating study of the relations between language and food in the Renaissance, see Michel Jeanneret's *A Feast of Words* (Chicago: University of Chicago Press, 1991).

9. I elaborate in greater detail on the relations between food and the representation of sexuality in devout literature, and especially in the writings of Saint François de Sales, in Chapter 4. The following passage is from an anonymous treatise on marriage inspired by the writings of De Sales and the devout spiritual tradition that spells out the model for devout marriage: "God, having established marriage to be the image of that of his son with the holy Church, and of the alliance of his very divine Word with human nature, wishes married people to *express* and *represent* in their particular behavior these divine prototypes . . . Now, as the son of God, in contracting an alliance with human nature, took the path of childhood, your devotion, to be in conformity with your state, should *put you to honoring* these two great mysteries: the Childhood of Jesus and his mystical Marriage with the Holy Church, through the *adorations of love* and through the *union of spirit with grace* of these august mysteries." Quoted in H. Brémond, *Histoire littéraire du sentiment religieux en France,* vol. 9 (Paris: Armand Colin, 1967), p. 298; my translation.

10. Memnon's tomb is described in the following terms: "He was interred in a black tomb, with an epitaph *to give to his memory the image of life*" (pp. 38–39).

11. Memnon, in vase paintings, is usually given heroic features. A favorite theme in archaic and classical vase-painting depicts Memnon's final combat and his body carried away by his mother. This detail, I believe, reinforces his symbolic identification with Jesus in Camus's text.

2. According to Bremond, "Camus sait Virgile par coeur" ("Camus knows Virgil by heart"), *Histoire littéraire du sentiment religieux en France*, I, 150. The Dido Camus is invoking here, however, is not the Dido of the Aeneid. Dido is the chaste queen described in Boccaccio's *De casibus virorum illustrium,* translated by L. Brewer Hall as *The Fates of Illustrious Men* (New York: Ungar Press, 1965): "After a short time this city increased in population because of its very favorable situation, and here, making the laws, queenly Dido ruled with complete justice. She lived as a very honorable widow, observing the sacred virtue of chastity. And thus she achieved her desire" (pp. 54–57).

13. The last story of the *Decameron* is devoted to Griselda, and Perrault, in his *Contes* (Paris: Gallimard, [1697], 1981), devotes a short story to the patient Griseldis.

14. *History of the Franks,* trans. Lewis Thorperk (New York: Penguin, 1974), II, 34, 149–150.

15. Cicero, *Tusculan Disputations* (Cambridge, Mass.: Harvard University Press/Loeb Classical Library, 1971), III, XXXI.74–76. Fontenelle, in his *Nouveaux dialogues des morts* (Paris: Marcel Didier, [1683], 1971), presents a different Artemisia:

"*Artemisia: I* resemble *you!* I, who was a model of conjugal fidelity, who drank the ashes of my husband, who built him a superb monument admired by the whole world! How could I resemble a man who spent his life looking for the secret of turning metals into gold?

Raymond Lulle: Yes, yes, I know very well what I'm talking about. After all the fine things you have just boasted of, you became enamored of a young man who didn't love you. You sacrified to him this magnificent building from which you could have derived so much glory; and the ashes of Mausoleus that you drank were not a sufficient remedy to a new passion.

Artemisia: I didn't think you were so well informed of my affairs. This part of my life is little known, and I didn't imagine that there were people who knew of it.

Raymond Lulle: You will admit then that our destinies do have some relationship, in that we are both given honor that we don't deserve. For you, to believe that you were always faithful to the memory of your husband, and for me, that I had succeeded in the Great Work.

Artemisia: I admit it willingly. The public is made to be the dupe in many things. One must profit from what its propensities are." (pp. 310–318)

Artemisia's loyalty and her devotion to her dead husband are here presented as mere illusion. This view is echoed by a number of seventeenth-century French writers. For instance, Scudéry in one of his poems evokes Artemisia as a model and paradigm of mourning while warning against her alleged affair with a younger lover: "Epigram for Madame, the Dowager Princess / On the death of Monsieur, her husband / Imitate Artemisia in her fidelity; / Render the memory of your spouse immortal / By a great Monument, superb in its beauty, / Whose Model I draw here. / But don't imitate her the way she lost her clear vision, / And be more constant, being already more beautiful." *Poésies Diverses,* I (Paris: Nizet, 1983), 154; my translation.

Fénelon, in his *Dialogues sur l'éloquence* (Paris: Gallimard, 1983), strongly criticizes the use of the figure of Artemisia in Christian discourse and her identification with Christian religious figures: "Don't you see, monsieur? What is the point of being pleasant about such a frightening subject, or amusing the listener with the profane recital of the pain of Artemisia, when one should rage on about it and furnish nothing but terrible images of death?" (p. 6). In D. Bouhours's *La manière de bien penser dans les ouvrages d'esprit* (Amsterdam, 1705), we have an interesting description of Artemisia and the heart: "Salerius Maximus, speaking of the Artemisia who drank the funerary ashes of her husband, certainly called her a living tomb; and a gallant man of this century, even more illustrious because of his valor and virtue than because of his works, in order to build a mausoleum for the Queen Mother Anne of Austria, raised a Pyramid of flaming hearts with these Spanish words: *Assi Sepultada no es muerta*" (pp. 218–219). Finally, for a discussion of the fate of Artemisia at the end of the seventeenth century and her ambiguous status as a paradigm of mourning, as well as a critique of Cicero's analysis of her mourning, see Bayle's article devoted to her in his *Dictionnaire historique et critique* (Geneva: Slatkine Reprints,

[1697], 1969), II, 474–477. See also my "Du bon usage du deuil: Le cas d'Artémise," *Le Genre humain,* special issue on "Les Bons sentiments," 29 (1995), 139–148.

16. All references to La Ceppède are from *Les Théorèmes sur le Sacré Mystère de notre Rédemption, reproduction de l'édition de Toulouse de 1613-1622. Préface de Jean Rousset* (Geneva: Droz, 1966). English translations in the text are mine.

17. On this point see Yves Congar, *Etudes d'ecclésiologie médiévale* (London: Variorum Reprints, 1983), pp. 152–155 and 170–173.

18. This explanatory sonnet is found at the end of La Ceppède's volume in a collection of poems entitled *La Muse Grecque, Latine, et Française sur les Théorèmes de Messire Jean de la Ceppède.*

19. The attraction to the Eucharist is often associated with the desire to see it but also with its odor: "The spouse of Christ, compelled by the *odor* of this vivifying sacrament, had from her childhood to the end of her life the desire to see the blessed host." From the account describing the visions and teachings of Dorothy of Montau, written by John Marienwerder, quoted in C. Bynum, *Holy Feast and Holy Fast* (Berkeley: University of California Press, 1987), p. 55, emphasis added. For a general survey of the role of the Eucharist in the Middle Ages, see Miri Rubin, *Corpus Christi* (Cambridge: Cambridge University Press, 1991). In La Ceppède's *Théorèmes,* there is a sonnet (III, C) that develops the relations between the odor and the heart and tomb of Christ: "Never this hollow rock had in its enclosure / A dead body; it is virgin, it is new, and this is the reason / For giving to my Christ (who all of Nature / Surpasses in purity) a pure house. // But why aloe and myrrh aplenty / To embalm this body exempt from rot? / Why all these perfumes? In what is their vapor / Necessary to this sepulcher? // Let us spread, to teach us to perfume our hearts, / Thoughts and desires that conquer garbage / To serve as a venerable tomb for this death. // Dead one, who can alone perfume our desires / With your graces, great God, be favorable / To the great extent to which I breathe you into my heart."

20. Quoted in Janet Tibbetts Schulenburg's "The Heroics of Virginity," in *Women in the Middle Ages and the Renaissance,* ed. Mary Beth Rose (Syracuse, N.Y.: Syracuse University Press, 1986), p. 42.

21. Camus's invocation of the figures of Joshua and Caleb has its origin in Gregory of Nyssa's *De vita Moys* [392], translated in French as *Vie de Moïse* (Paris: Albin Michel, 1993), p. 148; English translation mine: "But Moses, giving no weight to these contradictory discourses, sided with the one bringing good information onto the earth. Now, Joshua was the head of those bringing favorable news; he put his authority behind the faith in the promised things. Leaning in his direction, Moses had the firm hope for a future good, seeing an indication of the delights ahead in the cluster of grapes Joshua had brought suspended from poles. Hearing of Joshua who informs us about the country beyond and the grapes suspended from wood, you divine what it was that Moses saw that strengthened his hopes. The cluster suspended from wood; what is it, other than the grapes hanging from wood in the last days, whose blood becomes the drink of salvation for those who believe? In this, Moses enigmatically announces to us in advance that 'they drank the wine, the blood of the grape,' which signifies the salutory Passion."

4. *Elephantine Marriage and Devout Sexuality*

1. *Bestiary,* Harleian Manuscript 3244, British Museum, quoted in H. Williams, *Sacred Elephant* (London: Jonathan J. Cape, 1984), p. 163.
2. All references to the works of Saint François de Sales, unless otherwise specified, are to *Oeuvres* (Paris: Gallimard, 1969).
3. *Introduction à la vie dévote*, in *Oeuvres,* p. 240. The English translations come from *Introduction to the Devout Life,* trans. and ed. John K. Ryan (New York: Vintage Books, 1966), p. 226.
4. Saint François de Sales quotes directly from Pliny's *Natural History.* He selects the passage, however, that highlights the loyalty and the low sexual appetite of the elephant. Here is the full text of Pliny: "It is also because of modesty that they only couple in secret [*pudore numquam nisi in abdito coeunt*]: the male engenders when he is five years old, the female, ten. The female allows sexual contact only once every two years and, it is said, for five days a year, not more: the sixth day, the couples bathe in a river, and rejoin their herd only after the bath. They know no adultery, and do not engage each

other in mortal combat over females as do other animals; not because they do not know the power of love, for the tale is told of the elephant who was enamored of a salesgirl; and have no illusion that she was chosen by accident: she was the mistress of the famous grammarian Aristophanes. Another elephant was taken with Menander, a young Syracusan who served in Ptolemy's army, and when the elephant couldn't see him, he manifested his unhappiness by refusing to eat. Juba tells that a young perfume dealer was loved by one of them. They all gave proof of their affection: joy at the sight of the beloved, naïve caresses, coins that they were given were saved and showered into the lap of their loves. In fact, there is nothing surprising about animals so well endowed with memory showing such attachment." Pline L'Ancien, *Histoire Naturelle,* trans. A. Ernout (Paris: Belles Lettres, 1952), VIII:V:13, 27–28); English translation mine.

It is clear that Saint François omits the sections describing the elephant as a lover or at least as an animal with lust; he also speaks only of the behavior of the bull elephant, neglecting entirely the female elephant or the behavior of couples. In the classical literature on the elephant, the jealousy of the elephant is rarely discussed. What we encounter, however, are discussions of cases in which an elephant is in love with a human female. Furthermore, the female elephant is curiously missing from most of the classical texts that deal with elephants. Aelian, in his *De Natura Animalium* (VIII, 17), describes instances of the jealousy of elephants. For a general survey of the classical representations of elephants, see H. H. Scullard's *The Elephant in the Greek and the Roman World* (Ithaca, N.Y.: Cornell University Press, 1974). For a discussion of *must* in elephants, see F. Edgerton, *The Elephant-Lore of the Hindus: The Elephant-Sport [Matanga-Lila] of Milakantha* (New Haven, Conn.: Yale University Press, 1931). On the *must* and the sexual symbolism of the elephant, see Wendy Doniger O'Flaherty, *Women, Androgynes, and Other Mythical Beasts* (Chicago: University of Chicago Press, 1980). On the relationship between the elephant and memory, see Charles Malamoud, *Cuire le monde* (Paris: La Découverte, 1989).

5. *Instruction sur le mariage* (Lyon, 1683), p. 89.

6. *Traité de l'amour de Dieu,* in *Oeuvres,* p. 627.

7. *Saint Bernard,* ed. E. Gilson (Paris: Presses Universitaires de France, 1949), p. 217; translation mine.

8. This text is echoed in Camus's "Le Coeur mangé" in the description of Crisele's parents' decision to marry her to Rogat: "You think that such just passions can be taken off as easily as a dress, and that you can deal with their captive affections as if they were free? But they are supposed to have no inclination or choice other than the wishes of their parents. Would that it were as easy to do so as it is to say so. But experience shows that these propositions don't always have the conclusions we might think. Do you want to control animals that are sold or rented out to anyone? You push them toward the precipice and want them to hold back; you allow them inclinations and then want them to be indifferent; you throw them into the fire and then don't want them to feel the flames? Do you take them for the Pyralides, who live in furnaces without being consumed?" (31–32).

9. Villars de Montfaucon (1635–1673), *Le comte de Gabalis ou Entretiens sur les Sciences secrètes* (London: B. Lintott and E. Curll, 1714), p. 128; translation mine. The image of the butterfly representing the drive of the mystical soul is common in all religious traditions. One example taken from a Moslem source can be found in Louis Massignon, *The Passion of al-Hallaj,* trans. Herbert Mason (Princeton: Princeton University Press, 1982), II, 54: "Now, know that mansur Hallaj, God hold him in his mercy, was in the audience of His glorious majesty like a butterfly before a candle. The moth that sees a candle in the night imagines it to be a shining star; it goes toward it, and rushes into the flame, wanting to taste the full brightness of the candle; but it is immediately set on fire without succeeding in grasping a particle of light, and it falls, burned, before the taper: it realizes its powerlessness then and confesses: 'I who had thought I could be something in the presence of light now know that I am nothing.' And as soon as it has recognized its powerlessness, its eyes open and it sees the top of the taper, lopped off and fallen down beside it. That is to say, that from the moment it has realized its lowness and humbled itself, it reaches its Goal. Hallaj, in the same way, had imagined he could be something in

the audience of the Divinity when he had perceived its light. Once burned, he recognized his lowness, and, in the same way, he reached his Goal." (From *Kitab anis al-jalis wa nadim al-ra'is* by Abu'l-Farj Nahrawli.)

10. For a discussion of Binet's *Attraits*, see Henri Bremond's *Histoire littéraire du sentiment religieux en France* (Paris: Armand Colin, 1968).

11. *Des Attraits tout puissants de l'amour de Jesus-Christ* (Paris, 1631), p. 549; English translations are mine.

12. Ibid., p. 560. Binet's association of the Eucharist with a discussion of the Virgin echoes some commentary by Gregory of Nyssa on the subject in his *De vita Moys*: "But the body of this bread (manna) is produced neither by sowing nor labor. The earth, unchanging, found itself covered with this divine food that those who are hungry eat: this is the mystery of the Virgin, taught to us in advance through this miracle. This bread, which is not the product of the earth, is also Word" (104).

13. For instance, see Charles Perrault, *Parallèle des Anciens et des Modernes* (Geneva: Slatkine Reprints, [1697], 1979), I, 234 and II, 164–165.

14. Marivaux, *Journaux et Oeuvres diverses* (Paris: Classiques Garnier, 1988).

15. Ibid., pp. 68–70; my translation.

16. The story is preceded by a number of chapters that are devoted to the description and analysis of what de Sales calls the "suprême effet de l'amour affectif" ("supreme effect of affective love"), that is, the death of the mystical lovers: "Sacred love is indeed so violent that its effects cause the separation of body and soul, causing its lovers to die a very happy death worth more than a hundred lives." *Traité de l'amour de Dieu*, p. 690.

17. In fact, the story signals a return to a rich topos in medieval hagiography.

18. The story combines a number of elements widely present in medieval literature. For a general survey of the literature, see Marie Anne Polo de Beaulieu, "La légende du coeur inscrit dans la littérature religieuse et didactique," in *Le CUER au Moyen Age* (Aix: Presses

Universitaires d'Aix, 1991), pp. 299–312. The story reworks a number of texts that narrate the visits of noblemen and knights to the Holy Land as well as saints' lives, especially Saint Ignatius and Saint Bernardino of Sienna.

19. The inscription recalls the story of the death of Saint Ignatius: "We read furthermore that Saint Ignatius, in the middle of so many torments, ceaselessly invoked the name of Jesus Christ. When his torturers asked him why he repeated this name so often, he said, 'This name, I carry it inscribed in my heart; this is the reason that I cannot stop invoking it.' Now, after his death, those who had heard him speak thus wanted to be sure of the fact; they therefore took his heart out of his body, and cutting it in two, found these words engraved in gold in the middle: Jesus Christ." Jacques de Voragine, *La Légende dorée* (Paris: Garnier Flammarion, [1264], 1970), I, 187; my translation.

20. The conclusion of the *Traité de l'amour de Dieu* will emphasize the central role of the heart and its relation to the Passion for the mystic: "And finally, in conclusion, the Death and Passion of Our Lord is the sweetest and most violent motive that can animate our hearts in this mortal life: and it is true that mystical bees make their most excellent honey in the wounds of this *Lion of the tribe of Juda,* whose throat was cut, who was torn asunder on Mount Calvary; and the children of the Cross glory in their admirable problem, that the world does not understand: that out of death, which devours everything, comes the meat of our consolation" (970–971).

5. Trials and Tribulations of the Human Heart

1. Saint Bonaventure, *Les Six jours de la Création*, trans. Marc Ozilou (Paris: Desclée/Cerf, 1991), I, 19–20, 112–113; English translation mine.

2. Adrien Baillet, *Vie de Monsieur Descartes* (Paris: Table Ronde, 1946 [1692]), p. 11; my translation.

3. *Moralistes du XVII Siècle,* ed. Jean Lafond (Paris: Robert Laffont, 1992), pp. 232–233; my translations.

4. La Rochefoucauld, in his *Avis au Lecteur* in the first edition of the

Maximes, tries to situate but also to distance his *Réflexions* from the Church Fathers' writings. In describing the letter that accompanies the *Avis,* La Rochefoucauld claims that "the letter suffices to show that what they contain is nothing other than the digest of a morality conforming to the thoughts of several of the Church Fathers . . ." *Moralistes,* p. 232.

5. *Moralistes,* pp. 350–351.

Selected Bibliography

Abraham, N., and M. Torok. *L'écorce et le noyau*. Paris: Aubier-Flammarion, 1978.

Adam, Antoine. *Histoire de la littérature française au XVIIème siècle*. Paris: Editions Mondiales, 1962.

Andry, F. *Recherches sur le coeur et le foie considérés aux points de vue littéraire, médico-historique, symbolique, etc.* Paris, 1858.

Anon. *Instruction sur le mariage*. Lyon, 1683.

Ariès, Philippe. *The Hour of Our Death,* trans. Helen Weaver. New York: Vintage Books, 1982 (1977).

Aristotle. *De Motu Animalium,* trans. Martha Nussbaum. Princeton, N.J.: Princeton University Press, 1978.

d'Aubigné, Agrippa. *Les Tragiques*. Paris: Garnier Flammarion, 1968.

Augustine, Saint. *City of God*. New York: Penguin Books, 1984.

Bacon, Francis. *The Essays,* ed. with an intro. by John Pitcher. New York: Penguin, 1985.

Baillet, Adrien. *Vie de Monsieur Descarte*s. Paris: La Table Ronde, 1946 (1692).

Bayle, P. *Dictionnaire historique et critique*. Geneva: Slatkine Reprints, [1697+], 1969.

Beaujeu, Renaut de. *Le Lai d'Ignaure ou lai du prisonnier,* ed. Rita Lejeune. Brussels: Palais des Académies, 1938.

Beaulieu, Marie Anne Polo de. "La légende du coeur inscrit dans la littérature religieuse et didactique," in *Le CUER au Moyen Age*. Aix: Presses Universitaires d'Aix, 1991.

Benveniste, Emile. *Vocabulaire des institutions Indo-Européennes*. Paris: Minuit, 1969.

Binet, Etienne. *Des Attraits tout puissants de l'amour de Jesus-Christ*. Paris, 1631.

Blackman, A. M. *The Literature of the Ancient Egyptians*. New York: Arno Books, 1977.

Boccaccio, G. *De casibus virorum illustrium*, trans. by L. Brewer Hall as *The Fates of Illustrious Men*. New York: Ungar Press, 1965.

———— *The Decameron*, trans. John Payne, rev. and ed. Charles Singelton. Berkeley: University of California Press, 1982.

Bodenstedt, M. I. *The "Vita Christi" of Ludolphus the Carthusian*. Washington, D.C.: Catholic University Press, 1944.

Bouhours, D. *La manière de bien penser dans les ouvrages d'esprit*. Amsterdam, 1705.

Boyadijan, N. *Le Coeur: Son histoire, son symbolisme, son iconographie et ses maladies*. Anvers: Esco Books, 1980.

Brémond, H. *Histoire littéraire du sentiment religieux en France*. Paris: Armand Colin, 1967.

Burke, N. *Homo Necans: The Anthropology of Ancient Greek Sacrificial Ritual and Myth*, trans. Peter Bing. Berkeley: University of California Press, 1983 (1972).

Bynum, Caroline. *Holy Feast and Holy Fast*. Berkeley: University of California Press, 1987.

Camus, Jean-Pierre. *L'Amphithéâtre sanglant* (1630).

———— *Le Bouquet d'histoires agréables* (1662).

———— *Les Leçons exemplaires* (1632).

———— *Les Occurences remarquables* (1628).

———— *Les Rencontres funestes* (1644).

———— *Les Spectacles d'Horreur. Avec une introduction de René Godenne*. Geneva: Slatkine Reprints, 1973.

———— *La Tour des miroirs* (1631).

———— *Le Verger historique* (1644).

Chandlery, S. J. *Friends and Apostles of the Sacred Heart of Jesus*. New York, 1915.

Selected Bibliography

Cicero. *Tusculan Disputations.* Cambridge, Mass.: Harvard University Press/Loeb Classical Library, 1971.

Collet, J. *La dévotion au Sacré Coeur de Jésus établie et réduite en pratique.* Paris, 1770.

Congar, Y. *Etudes d'ecclésiologie médiévale.* London: Variorum Reprints, 1983.

Croiset, S. J. *La dévotion au sacré coeur.* Lyon, 1741.

Coulanges, Fustel de. *The Ancient City.* Baltimore: Johns Hopkins University Press, 1980 (1864).

Dante. *La vita nuova. Edizione nazionale delle opere di Dante,* vol. I, ed. M. Barbi. Florence: Bemporad, 1932.

Dante's Vita Nuova, trans. M. Musa. Bloomington: University of Indiana Press, 1973.

Delatte, A. *La Catopromancie et ses dérivés.* Paris: E. Droz, 1932.

Dentzer, J.-M. *Le motif du banquet couché dans le Proche-Orient et le Monde Grec du Vii au IV siècle avant J.-C.* Paris: Ecole Française de Rome, 1982.

Descrains, Jean, ed. Jean-Pierre Camus, *Homélies des Etats Généraux.* Paris: Droz, 1970.

Detienne, Marcel. *Dionysos mis à mort.* Paris: Gallimard, 1987.

Doré, A. *Le sacré Coeur et le vénérable Jean Eudes.* Paris: Hachette, 1891.

Doresse, J. "Le coeur et les anciens égyptiens." *Etudes Carmélitaines* 29 (1950).

Dubois, E. "Some interpretations of the notion of *coeur* in 17th-century France." *Seventeenth-Century French Studies* IX (1987).

Dufau, P. *Trésor du Sacré Coeur de Jésus,* 8 vols. Brussels, 1870.

Edgerton, F. *The Elephant-Lore of the Hindus: The Elephant-Sport [Matanga-Lila] of Milakantha.* New Haven: Yale University Press, 1931.

Erman, A. *Die Literatur der Aegypter.* Leipzig: J. C. Hinrichs, 1923.

Favret, R. *Trente Nouvelles de Jean-Pierre Camus.* Paris: Vrin, 1977.

Fénelon, F. de S. *Oeuvres I.* Paris: Gallimard, 1983.

Ferguson, G. *Signs and Symbols in Christian Art.* New York: Oxford University Press, 1966.

Fontenelle, B. le B. *Nouveaux dialogues des morts.* Paris: Marcel Didier, [1683], 1971.

Furley, David F. *Galen's On Respiration and the Arteries*. Princeton, N.J.: Princeton University Press, 1984.

Godenne, R. *Histoire de la Nouvelle Française aux XVII et XVIII siècles*. Geneva: Droz, 1970.

Gregory of Nyssa. *De vita Moys* [392]. Translated as *Vie de Moïse*. Paris: Albin Michel, 1993.

Gregory of Tours. *History of the Franks*, trans. Lewis Thorperk. New York: Penguin, 1974.

Guiraud, P. *Sémiologie de la sexualité*. Paris: Payot, 1978.

Hadot, P. "Le mythe de Narcisse et son interpretation par Plotin." *Nouvelle Revue de Psychanalyse* 13 (1976).

Hainsworth, G. *Les "Novelas Exemplares" de Cervantes en France au XVIIe siècle*. Paris: Champion, 1933.

Harris, C. R. S. *The Heart and the Vascular System in Ancient Greek Medicine*. New York: Oxford University Press, 1973.

Harrison, R. P. *The Body of Beatrice*. Baltimore: Johns Hopkins University Press, 1988.

Hyde, T. *The Poetic Theology of Love*. Newark, N.J.: Rutgers University Press, 1986.

Jeanneret, M. *A Feast of Words*. Chicago: University of Chicago Press, 1991.

Kantorowicz, Ernst. *The King's Two Bodies: A Study in Medieval Political Theology*. Princeton, N.J.: Princeton University Press, 1957.

Keller, J. *The Sacred Heart*. New York, 1899.

La Ceppède. *Les Théorèmes sur le Sacré Mystère de notre Rédemption, reproduction de l'édition de Toulouse de 1613–1622. Préface de Jean Rousset*. Geneva: Droz, 1966.

Lafond, Jean, ed. *Moralistes du XVIIème siècle*. Paris: Laffont, 1992.

Le Coeur. Etudes Carmélitaines 29 (1950).

Le coeur mangé: Récits érotiques et courtois des XIIème et XIIème siècles. Paris: Stock, 1979.

Le Goff, Jacques. *Pour un autre Moyen âge: Temps, travail et culture en Occident*. Paris: Gallimard, 1977.

——— *La bourse et la vie*. Paris: Hachette, 1986.

Lefebvre, Gustave. *Romans et contes égyptiens de l'époque Pharaonique*. Paris: Maisonneuve, 1949.

Lestringant, Frank. "Catholiques et Cannibales: Le thème du cannibalisme dans le discours protestant au temps des Guerres de religion," in *Pratiques et Discours Alimentaires à la Renaissance.* Paris: Maisonneuve et Larose, 1982.

Lewinshon, R. *Histoire entière du coeur: Erotisme. Symbolisme. Chirurgie. Physiologie. Psychologie.* Paris: Plon, 1962.

Lichtheim, Miriam. *Ancient Egyptian Literature,* vol. II. Berkeley: University of California Press, 1976.

Malaise, Michel. *Les scarabées de coeur dans l'Egypte ancienne.* Brussels: Fondation Egyptologique Reine Elisabeth, 1978.

Malamoud, Charles. *Cuire le monde.* Paris: La Découverte, 1989.

Marivaux, P. *Journaux et Oeuvres diverses.* Paris: Classiques Garnier, 1988.

Maspero, G. *Les Contes populaires de l'égypte ancienne.* Paris: Maisonneuve, 1911.

Massignon, Louis. *The Passion of al-Hallaj,* trans. Herbert Mason. Princeton, N.J.: Princeton University Press, 1982.

Matzke, John E. "The Legend of the Eaten Heart." *Modern Language Notes* 26:1 (1911).

Montaigne, M. *Essais.* Paris: Presses Universitaires de France, 1965.

Montfaucon, Villars de. *Le comte de Gabalis ou Entretiens sur les Sciences secrètes.* London: B. Lintott and E. Curll, 1742.

Muscatine, Charles. *The Old French Fabliaux.* New Haven: Yale University Press, 1986.

Nolan, B. "The *Vita Nuova:* Dante's Book of Revelation." *Dante Studies* 88 (1970).

O'Flaherty, Wendy Doniger. *Women, Androgynes, and Other Mythical Beasts.* Chicago: University of Chicago Press, 1980.

Paris, G. "Le conte du trésor du roi Rhampsinite." *Revue de l'Histoire des Religions* 55 (1907) .

Patzig, H. *Zur Geschichte des Herzmäre.* Berlin, 1891.

Pépin, J. "Plotin et le miroir de Dionysos." *Revue Internationale de Philosophie* 24 (1970).

——— *Théologie cosmique et théologie chrétienne.* Paris: Presses Universitaires de France, 1964.

Perrault, Charles. *Les Hommes illustres.* Paris: Antoine Dezallier, 1696.

——— *Parallèle des Anciens et des Modernes.* Geneva: Slatkine Reprints, [1697], 1979.

Petrovits, J. J. *Theology of the Cult of the Sacred Heart.* Washington, D.C.: Catholic University Press, 1917.

Piankoff, Alexandre. *Le Coeur dans les textes égyptiens depuis l'Ancien Empire jusqu'à la fin du Nouvel Empire.* Paris: Presses Universitaires de France, 1930.

Plotinus. *On Beauty.* Cambridge, Mass.: Harvard University Press/Loeb Classical Library, 1966.

Plutarch. *Moralia XIII.* Cambridge, Mass.: Harvard University Press/Loeb Classical Library, 1969.

Proclus. *Commentary on Plato's Parmenides,* trans. G. R. Morrow and J. M. Dillon. Princeton, N.J.: Princeton University Press, 1987.

Réau, L. *Iconographie de l'art chrétien,* 6 vols. Paris: Presses Universitaires de France, 1955–1959.

Rose, Mary Beth, ed. *Women in the Middle Ages and the Renaissance.* Syracuse, N.Y.: Syracuse University Press, 1986.

Rubin, Miri. *Corpus Christi.* Cambridge: Cambridge University Press, 1991.

Saint Bernard, ed. E. Gilson. Paris: Presses Universitaires de France, 1949.

Saint Bonaventure. *Les Six jours de la Création,* trans. Marc Ozilou. Paris: Desclée/Cerf, 1991.

Saint François de Sales. *Oeuvres.* Paris: Gallimard, 1969.

——— *Introduction to the Devout Life,* trans. and ed. John K. Ryan. New York: Vintage Books, 1966.

Sauvy, A. *Le miroir du coeur.* Paris: Cerf, 1989.

Scudéry, G. *Poésies Diverses,* I. Paris: Nizet, 1983.

Scullard, H. H. *The Elephant in the Greek and the Roman World.* Ithaca, N.Y.: Cornell University Press, 1974.

Simpson, William Kelly, ed. *The Literature of Ancient Egypt: An Anthology of Stories, Instructions, and Poetry.* New Haven: Yale University Press, 1972.

Sozzi, Lionello, ed. *La Nouvelle française à la Renaissance.* Geneva: Slatkine, 1981.

Spivak, G. C. "Finding Feminist Readings: Dante-Yeats." *Social Text* 2 (1980).

Vauchez, André. *La sainteté en Occident aux derniers siècles du moyen âge.* Paris: Ecole Française de Rome, 1981.

Vernant, J.-P. *L'individu, la mort, l'amour en grèce ancienne.* Paris: Gallimard, 1989.

de Voragine, Jacques. *La Légende dorée.* Paris: Garnier Flammarion, [1264], 1970.

Wallace, Howard N. *The Eden Narrative,* Harvard Semitic Monographs. Atlanta: Scholars' Press, 1985.

West, M. L. *The Orphic Poems.* New York: Oxford University Press, 1983.

Williams, H. *Sacred Elephant.* London: Jonathan J. Cape, 1984.

Index

Index

.